CW00393151

THE RUNNER'S NUTS

Tales of Tenacity and Training!

By the author of
FARTLEKS AND FLATULENCE
DAVID BERRIDGE

Published in 2016 by Dave Berridge
www.daveberridge.co.uk

Printed by Crossprint.co.uk

List of Adventures, Marathon Distance and above

1: The Marathon Des Sables 1996

2: The London Marathon 1997

3: The Himalayan 100 stage race 1998

4: The London Marathon 1998

5: The London Marathon 1999

6: Snowdonia Marathon 1999

7: Isle of Wight Marathon 2000

8: Hi Tec Adventure Race 2000

9: The Jordan Desert Cup 2001

10: Trail Plus Adventure Race 2002

11: The Raid Amazonie 2003

12: The Three Peaks Challenge 2003

13: The Guadarun 2004

14: The London Marathon 2004

15: Climbed Kilimanjaro 2004

16: Treadmill Challenge (100 miles in 24 hours) 2004

17: Paris Marathon 2005

18: 7X7X7 (7 marathons in 7 days and 7 different ways) 2005

19: Jersey Challenge Adventure Race 2005

20: Yukon Arctic Ultra 100 miles 2006

21: West Wight Triathlon 2006

22: Dublin City Marathon 2006

23: Wight Challenge Adventure Race 2006

24: Yukon Arctic Ultra 320 miles 2007

25: Ironman UK 70.3 2007

26: Tough Guy 2007

27: 6633 Ultra 2008 (DNF)

28: Atacama Crossing 2009

29: Norseman Extreme Triathlon 2010 (DNF)

30: Augrabies Extreme Ultra Marathon 2010

31: Brighton Marathon 2010

32: Yukon Arctic Ultra 430 miles 2011

33: Caesars Camp 100 mile Endurance Run 2011 (DNF)

34: North Downs Way 50 miler 2012

35: Winter 100 mile Ultra 2012 (DNF)

36: Namib Desert Challenge 2012

37: 6633 Ultra 352 miler 2013

38: Arrowhead 135 2014

39: Siberian Ice Marathon 2015

40: The Gobi March 2015

41: Rovaniemi 150 2016

42: 10 Ultra Marathons in 10 days 2016

The Runner's Nuts

Contents

2	List of Adventures, Marathon Distance and above
8	Chapter 1 The Tough Guy
19	Chapter 2 Arrowhead 135
39	Chapter 3 Caesar's Camp Endurance Run
57	Chapter 4 The Siberian Ice Marathon
71	Chapter 5 The Gobi March
113	Chapter 6 My First Marathon
121	Chapter 7 Training
143	Chapter 8 What it takes!
151	Chapter 9 Why on Earth!
157	Chapter 10 Physical Pain
161	Chapter 11 How things have changed
165	Chapter 12 Miscellaneous
167	Chapter 13 A few things I've learnt
175	Chapter 14 Rovaniemi 150
193	Chapter 15 The Last Chapter
196	Acknowledgements
197	Also by the Author

In 1996 David took part in what was then described as the 'Toughest Footrace on Earth' the world famous 'Marathon Des Sables' – a challenging 150 mile running race across the Sahara Desert.

In 2016, some twenty years later, and twenty years of competing in the toughest races he can find, he is still racing and still enjoys the crazy sport of Ultra Distance Running.

The 'Runner's Nuts' attempts to look at the how and the why – why a very ordinary bloke with an ordinary job chooses to take part, and often succeeds, in the extraordinary sport of Ultra Distance Running.

It looks at how he has managed to remain enthusiastic about the sport and, more importantly, how he has remained injury-free after two decades of racing across some of the world's harshest environments such as the Arctic, deserts, mountains and jungles. This ordinary 56 year old bloke attempts to explain his so-called training regime, a training regime that has allowed him to be both competitive and injury-free in the physically tough, demanding sport of Ultra Distance Running.

It looks at his personal nutritional philosophy and the psychology behind the sport – the 'what it takes' to compete for so long in the tough, physically demanding and mentally challenging world of Extreme Ultra Distance Racing.

Honest, thought-provoking and occasionally funny, 'The Runner's Nuts' is David's second book.

The Runner's Nuts

Chapter 1
The Tough Guy

What is it?:
An Obstacle Race

When?:
The last weekend in January

Where?:
Wolverhampton, England

Distance:
9 miles, 15 kms

It is:
A hoot, a mixture of madness and mayhem –
a must-do adventure

See:
www.toughguy.co.uk

These sort of novelty adventure races are great ways to break up the monotony of long, boring hours of training, for me they are a non-competitive, great all over body workout and, more importantly, something we can both do together.

On this occasion I can, without any fear what so ever, deny any responsibility for taking part in this 'crackers event'. Chivalry goes out the window, it was all my wife's fault, she made me do it. HONEST.

We were watching Channel 4 when a piece came on, showing slightly mad, terrified victims that were all either caked in crap, running through fire, leaping into an abyss and clambering over obstacles that had it all – it seemed to have been designed to humiliate and terrify, freeze and petrify.

Now, Mrs Berridge is normally the sensible one of the family. The one that tells me that I'm bonkers for wanting to run across the Arctic or take on an Ironman Triathlon when I can barely swim the length of the local pool and yet it was her who piped up with "I wouldn't mind having a go at that, do you fancy it?" No man in his right mind would have the balls to say, "No, it looks fucking awful, "when his wife says she's up for it, so, full of bravado and like a lamb to the slaughter, I lied and said, "Yep, it looks like a great fun challenge!"

Normally, when I sign up for some mad adventure, I register, pay, secure my place and then and only then do I think oh shit! What the hell have I done, this is madness, now I've gone and done it. This Tough Guy malarky was different I was actually thinking, oh shit, as the last syllable left my mouth.

Tough Guy can arguably claim to be the original and the best Obstacle race in the country, established in 1987 by an ex-guardsman Billy Wilson to raise funds for his few rescued horses, at the Tettenhall Horse Sanctuary. Billy is one of those colourful characters who realised early on that people are daft enough to pay good money to take part in a stupidly- challenging challenge. He also realised that by using the word Tough in the, title people would want to have a bash, each year he made the event a little more challenging and by holding the Tough Guy in what is more than likely to be the coldest weekend of the year he would make an already challenging challenge just a bit more challenging.

The popularity of the now famous Tough Guy has since seen a plethora of obstacle races such as Tough Mudder, the Spartan Race, Mudstacle, Mud & Madness and Winter Warrior Extreme as well as a host of others, all fantastic fun and very definitely a challenge as opposed to a serious 'balls to the wall' race. I believe that it's the non-racing, pure fun aspect of obstacle races that have, over the last few years, seen obstacle racing grow and grow and which has now become big business with even its own magazine, Obstacle Race Magazine (see www.obstacleracemagazine.com) and range of clothing and accessories.

We were lucky in that, whilst looking at the website, we realised that there were, in fact two races, one in the winter and one in the summer. Mrs Berridge 'insisted' on doing the summer one, I managed to hide my disappointment, and it was only with the greatest reluctance that I decided to also do the sensible summer one.

Decision made, training done, booked and paid for, we made our way to Wolverhampton and the start line to one of the more fun races of my life.-

Once the car was parked, we followed the well signposted route to the registration area, loud speakers blaring out music and instructions. It was packed with thousands of overly excited, slightly nervous competitors/victims, people and supporters, the press, TV crews and catering stalls, emergency crews like the ever present St John Ambulance, soldiers, Fire Brigade and even a bagpipe band. It all made for a heady mixture, helped in no small part by the colourful characters that were actually taking part in the challenge. Spiderman was talking to Rambo, who was armed to the teeth with an inflatable assault rifle, two St Trinians schoolgirls were talking to a group of lads who were looking resplendent in leopard print leotards.

We picked our through the crowds and, with the loudspeakers giving out last-minute instructions, like, have you all signed your death warrant and don't forget to get your number chiselled onto your forehead.

Once we were numbered with big black marker pens, as opposed to the afore-mentioned hammer and chisel combo we were instructed to make our way to the starting area. We were corralled into an area reserved for us, the Wobblemuckers. Each group had their own names, Wetnecks and Wobblemuckers being just two. We squeezed in just below a large mound which the front group of serious-looking proper out-to-win racing snakes were on the top of.

Next to the group of would-be racers was a set of old medieval stocks, these stocks, it turned out, were to be used as they were originally designed to be used for 'torture and/or public humiliation'. Any indiscretion, genuine or not that the rather flamboyant race organiser/ringmaster Billy Walker had deemed to have taken place by some poor unfortunate victim were to be placed in the stocks for said humiliation. One victim was escorted from the starting area for the rather heinous crime of wearing a lime green ill-fitting 'mankini'. A strip of material that appeared to be the size and texture of dental floss, flattering it was not, funny it most certainly was.

Once all the stocks were filled and last-minute helpful advice dispensed, advice like if you break your neck don't go running to me, it's your own bloody fault for signing up and as a final reminder we were all informed that the real Tough Guys do the winter one in January, this summer one was for wimps. We were now officially wimps!

As we approached the mound, the bag piping got louder, the first wave was off, we inched closer until cresting the summit we could see before us. Hundreds of runners sprinting off into what appeared to be a battlefield with smoke grenades of various colours gently wafting through the course. This section was fittingly called the Killing Fields, we were soon running down the steep hill, fighting gravity, lest we fall over and then get trampled on by the many hundreds of runners behind.

Once we reached the bottom of the hill and fought our way through the multi-coloured smoke, we were able to make out the first of the many obstacles, hurdles, not the proper hurdles seen at athletic meetings, oh no, these were hurdles fashioned out of telegraph poles, all, it seemed, placed at various heights, by a drunk, with a rather warped sense of humour, the ad hoc, rather sporadic arrangement left you with the first of many decisions: over or under, me being tall went over all of them, Mrs Berridge, however, is a short arse just sort of mixed and matched her way through. Once they had been negotiated and the field of runners nicely split up, it was a short run through the waist- high stinging nettles, hence the name nettle warrior. We both agreed that we were glad that we were not in the first wave because they had already gone through and had at least the decency to flatten a path for us to follow without getting stung, much!

Once out of the stingers, it was up a steep incline then down a steep incline then up a steep incline and down a steep incline, this masochistic slalom repeated itself until we were all puffing and panting, with our heart rates through the roof and, for the first time, a silence descended – not one runner was capable of even the slightest profanity.

It was a merciful relief to be back on the flat ground and into the shade of the woods, the short respite was exactly that, short, before us there was cargo netting and large plastic drums. This section was called, for some unknown reason, the Ghurkha Grand National. The netting was easy, having done a few adventure races I knew the best way through was to go backwards and, with Mrs Berridge following closely, we made short work of the nets then large plastic-covered bales of hay, again these didn't cause too many problems. I leapt over and dragged Mrs Berridge rather unceremoniously over, this was not helped by the fact that she was laughing so much.

We carried on using a mixture of running, walking and crawling, crawling under barbed wire on ground that was anything but soft, scraped knees and elbows. Once through the other side, it was more clambering over climbing walls, mud-filled quagmires, more cargo netting that was now pinned to the ground, which made crawling difficult because anything that could get caught up and tangled would get caught up and tangled. The netting only ended with a drop into another water-filled trench, unfortunately this drop was a natural catchment area, with the poor unsuspecting victim snared, the netting became more like a spider's web spun to catch the unwary – once caught and tangled, the poor unfortunate victim inadvertently caused chaos, with so many people behind, a log jam of people occurred, panic ensued as the victim tried in vain to extricate themselves. Nine times out of ten this was done by another racer, not through an act of compassion, but more an act of desperation on the part of that so-called 'Good Samaritan' wanting to get past and get a bloody move on.

Once extracted, the poor unfortunate plopped into the water-filled trench, popped up, gasped for breath and clambered up the other side ready to start the whole process again.

Then it was onto the next challenge, named the Colditz Walls, these were a set of three walls that got progressively higher, the first was at 2 meters, then 3 then finally 4 – again, each of the runners all helped each other, it was very definitely 'we're in it together 'attitude.

Taking advantage of the short walk between obstacles, which was the ominously named 'behemoth'* (Mentioned in the bible, as a monster, large or powerful mythical entity.) This was the big daddy of them all, consisting of 4 x 30 foot high platforms separated by ropes, one for feet and one overhead for hands.

Once we reached the bottom of the Behemoth we had a short but welcome break courtesy of the queue that had assembled, we started climbing up to the first of the rope sections, whilst climbing I couldn't help but look at the rather chaotic comedy before us. Just about every technique was employed to cross the rope sections, only very few seemed to be successful. Once i reached the ropes, I employed the feet and hands facing the same way and slowly slid along, feet and hands sliding along. I was fortunate that it worked, once safely over the other side I turned and waited for Mrs Berridge, who adopted a similar style, only one of the Flintstones, either Barney Rubble or Fred, had now turned up and was close behind and the bloke in front of her adopted styles that were, to say the least, a little different, the two ropes were now going in six different directions as was the expression on Mrs Berridge's face. I'm not sure and could have been wrong, but I felt the language that my wife was using was anything but ladylike – she had just finished explaining to them the error of their ways when all three of them became, for a split second, horizontal, the top rope and bottom rope were for that split second lying side by side. All three were then unceremoniously dumped onto the safety netting below.

I had my own battle royal going, I was laughing so much and I was trying really trying to hide it, needles to say I failed miserably and got caught. However, I was fortunate that she was too knackered to tell me off, even too tired to give me one of her looks.

Off the Behemoth and through the Battle of the Somme, crawling beneath barbed wire, into water-filled muddy ditches, out the water/mud combination, only to be met a raging fire of burning hay bales.

Only when we survived the swinging ropes, clambering climbs, possible drowning and fiery furnace were we lucky enough to enter the Tyre Crawl, long dark tunnels created by using hundreds of tyres. We managed to somehow survive the tube of tyres, to then enter the strength sapping Swamp, a man made mud crossing, designed it seems to do nothing but drain the very last piece of energy, a shoe sucking quagmire of the mud that required a gargantuan effort just for the simple effort of putting one foot in front of the other, this was made even more knackering by the fact that we both laughing so much.

Fortunately there was a short semi sensible run to the next obstacle the Vietcong Torture Chamber Tunnels. These large concrete tubes were pitch black and slippery and a real effort to crawl through the fact that so many people were all trying to inch their through the thing, made the whole thing a little cosy, anyone suffering from claustrophobia would have really struggled, if you picked the right ones you were lucky, the wrong ones seemed to be at a slight angle which meant that not only were trying to crawl along but you were also trying to climb up, another little surprise in store for anyone picking the wrong tunnel, was that a couple of the underground tunnels had trapdoors above and, every so often, the door would open, a beam of daylight would light up the thing blind you and then overly-enthusiastic flour-bombers would throw bags of flour, self-raising or plain – either was used resulting in the poor unfortunate victim now caked in mud, sweat, flour and other assorted crap.

I came out of my tunnel just in time to watch my wife being manhandled out of a tunnel by a bloke wearing what would not have been out of place for someone who works in the city: collar and tie with a rather nifty blazer.

Looking like a rabbit caught in a car's headlights, she took a moment to gather her thoughts and get her bearings, we held hands and laughed our way to the next obstacle.

The monster 14 metre high Sky Walk and Paradise Climb – this one was not too difficult, climbing up was ok, well, would have been, had I not had the mentally-scarring image of looking up a hairy-arsed bloke's skirt, an image I will have to try and erase from memory. It was the walk across that could potentially be a problem, with a 14 metre drop, though it was certainly safe enough, if you fell, tripped or slipped you were going nowhere, however if you were uncomfortable with heights it was the simple fact that you could see the water so far below that would make it a massive challenge. We both got across without too much fuss, Mrs Berridge was, however, unusually quiet and only started to get, shall we say, 'apprehensive' on the climb down, shaking arms and shaking legs were, I decided, not conducive to descending the 14m – it was literally a white knuckle descent, so tight was she gripping the cargo netting that her knuckles were white.

Once safely down it was a slow, very slow meander to the next, the Splosh Pool. This so called splash pool was in fact exactly what the pirates did in days gone by, walk the plank, numerous scaffolding boards extended out and over a lake, the good thing was that so many people were right behind you that you had no choice but to go for it, no hesitating, you either jumped off or fell off, once in the water you moved out the way pretty quickly, lest the next poor unfortunate victim land on you. I jumped, sort of, hitting the water and immediately moved off, turning around to see where Mrs Berridge was, just in time to see her showing off her impressive array of multi-tasking skills, she could hold her nose, scream and shout various things in an entirely new and as yet unheard of language, whilst at the same time flailing her arms and legs. I was a very proud husband!

After a short swim to shore, we immediately jumped in to yet another water-filled trench that took us on to the next challenge, a contraption designed to make you go under water with the heart rate through the roof. Laboured breathing, we had to hold our breath and duck under 3 telegraph poles, normally this wouldn't be a problem but I was breathing so hard I could only hold my breath for a few seconds. Luckily, 3/4 seconds was all it took, but once out the other side I was breathing even harder, puffing and panting like a sixty-a-day smoker.

Walking slowly to the next obstacle, the Brandenburger Gate, a simple 40ft high vertical climbing wall, once this was safely negotiated, it was onto the Death Plunge, this seemed to be a simple walkway of 10 inch planks across a lake. However, you never know, with a name like DEATH PLUNGE it could have been sulphuric acid, a lake filled with piranha, leeches or any other such nasties all designed to keep you guessing.

This was then followed by a short walk, well, for us anyway, onto the Jesus Bridge, a wobbly bridge made from floating barrels and planks. I could only guess the name Jesus Bridge was because when trying to cross the thing, all sort of blasphemous expletives were used.

More cargo netting, before we reached the Dragon Pools, this was a series of ropes stretched across a large lake, again it was a simple choice, either do a repeat performance of the rather slow slightly disastrous Behemoth or just jump into the water and swim/wade across – we both went for the swim/wade option.

Clambering up and out of the water and on to the next challenge, the Stalag Escape which involved crawling though mud and crap whilst trying not to get snagged on the very 'barbed' wire once a successful escape had been made, there was no time to rest. The Tyre Torture beckoned, a series of randomly laid out tyres, which was fine for people with little feet and great coordination. I, on the other hand have feet that are just slightly too big to fit inside the tyre so had to try and walk on wet, slippery rubber. Mrs Berridge enjoyed the fact that I now rather resembled an intoxicated Bambi, all legs, arms and very little dignity.

Then it was a case of crossing a small bridge and then taking on the Anaconda, a set of large concrete pipes that were difficult enough to clamber over, but the Anaconda came with an added bonus: dangling electric wires that, when touched, gave an electric shock or what could be better considered a preverbal kick up the arse.

Then onto the Viagra Falls, a steep, very steep muddy hillslide that once again required us to get electrocuted with more overhanging sadistic electrocution devices.

With the end tantalisingly close, it was just a question of entering the Torture Chamber a long, dark partially-flooded tunnel, the stuff of nightmares, groping and grabbing our way through. We emerged victorious, well not quite there was another short run, with a steep fell runners dream of a climb before sliding down a huge water slide whilst being hosed down by overly-enthusiastic race crew. Then a short sprint (sort of) to the finish line banner.

As we crossed the finish line, collected our medals and the even more important cup of tea and biscuits, our thoughts turned to the winter version. Shall we or shan't we?

ABSOLUTELY NOT, NO WAY, NOT EVER, EVER AGAIN (but we'll see!)

The Tough Guy is a brilliant fun-filled day, testing just about every kind of phobia there is, from acrophobia, claustrophobia, aquaphobia. I'm sure there were a few more.

We both loved it, great fun and an even greater work out.

Those guys and girls who do the winter version are truly crackers, where as we are just slightly crackers!

Chapter 2
Arrowhead 135

What is it?:
A multi-discipline, cold weather Ultra Distance race,
either bike, run or ski.

When?:
January

Where?:
Northern Minnesota, America

Distance:
135 miles (217km)

It is:
Deceptively tough

See:
www.arrowheadultra.com

Looking out of the aircraft window at the vast expanse of the Northern Minnesota wilderness, I again realised how lucky I was to be able to take part in yet another amazing race, or at least what I hoped would be an amazing race.

One question I was asking myself was, why? Why was I doing the Arrowhead 135? I had heard and read a lot about this race, it has a reputation for being brutal with a high dropout rate. Last year, (2013) out of the 40 runners, only 7 made it to the finish line. Though not particularly long at 135 miles, temperatures average around the -20/25 degrees and the course profile shows some small rolling hills. I was intrigued, curiosity, I had decided, had got the better of me.

Arriving at International Falls in Northern Minnesota, I made my way to the race-kit check in area. Confident in my kit choice, I made my way over to the table and laid my kit out and was interrogated to within an inch of my life. Questioned about calories, sleeping bag, gloves, even my fuel bottle was checked (he actually sniffed the fuel to make sure it was real!)

I now wish that I hadn't kept such a low profile. Having taken part in some pretty tough races in the Arctic before, I had chosen not to mention my experience. Consequently, they assumed I was racing in these conditions for the first time – this was not helped by the fact, that when asked about my training, I happened to mention that it had been a little difficult as this was the first snow I had seen this year. They had obviously decided that the 'limey' was a buffoon who was hopelessly out of his depth, comments like "It usually takes two or three attempts before finally nailing this race" and the dropout rate was high, seemed to confirmed this opinion.

In the book The Worlds Toughest Endurance Challenges by Richard Hoad and Paul Moore, the Arrowhead 135 is described as being brutally cold and fantastically raw, the Arrowhead 135 is as much about survival as it is about completing the gruelling 135-mile course.

After the kit check was completed, I packed up my kit and began to think to myself. Was I really out of my depth, was the Arrowhead 135 really that tough? Listening to the doom and gloom merchants talking about previous failed attempts, harsh conditions, tough terrain and horrendous hills, stories of frostbite and equipment failure, all I needed now was

for Private Fraser, the dour scotsman in Dads Army to come in and say that that we were "all doomed" and my rapidly-diminishing confidence would have, once and for all, been utterly diminished.

As I walked back to my hotel, I pondered the task in hand, pondered on what the other competitors had said and I then thought about my last two Arctic races. The tough, unforgiving Yukon Arctic Ultra, a 430 mile race from Whitehorse to Dawson, a race that saw just the 4 of us making it to the finish line. I remembered last year's 352 mile 6633 Ultra which, again, saw just 4 people reaching the finish-line, with me actually winning it.

I needed to put the Arrowhead into perspective, even if it was as tough as those last two races, the race cut off time would mean that I would only be suffering, miserable and or pissed off for a maximum two and a half days or 60 hours. The realisation that I only had to put up with any amount of suffering and any amount of misery for just 60 hours cheered me up, so rather than the impending dread, it was now a case of bring it on!

Back at the hotel, I got down to the serious business of packing my pulk. After five or six Arctic races, you would think that I was a dab hand at packing a pulk but, as per usual, I packed, unpacked and repacked and it was only the fact that time was ticking by and I had to be up early in the morning, that made me stop faffing about with the bloody thing.

I had arranged for a 05:00 wake up call, set my alarm and went to bed, hoping that I would hear the alarm call.

The start was at the Kerry Arena, a 20 minute drive from the hotel. Fortunately, the kindly assistant hotel manager offered to take both me and my sledge to the start. Unfortunately, it was whilst loading and lifting my sledge into the back of the vehicle, that the guy helping me slipped and nearly dropped my sledge. I caught the thing but, in doing so, slipped on the icy surface. I felt a twinge, a slight but very real twinge in my lower back, one of those sharp, stabbing pains that require a quick intake of breath and an instant rub. Trying to sit still in the car for the short journey was just about impossible. I was very uncomfortable and more than a little concerned. I eased my way out of the passenger side and realised that my right knee was a little uncomfortable. Trying not to let anyone see that I was in a little discomfort, I slid, rather than lifted, my sledge out of the back and thanked the driver, who wished me good luck.

Registration done, a quick wee and I made my way over to the start line. I was still being checked by the support crew, who wanted to make sure that my number was visible on the front, checked to see that I had the required amount of reflective material visible and then they checked to make sure that I had the right amount of red flashing lights blinking away. I got to the start line just in time to see the cyclists start, disappearing blinking red lights reflecting off the snow. It was certainly one of the noisier starts that I had experienced. Subdued silence, I noticed, is one thing that the Americans don't do very well.

Our countdown began – 3, 2, 1 and we were off. The trail was good: flat, wide and-well defined. The cyclists were slowly pulling away and the runners were jostling for position. The hundreds of little red flashing lights ahead were hypnotic but anyone suffering from photosensitive epilepsy would have been in real trouble.

The cyclists, as expected, pulled away quite quickly, the specially designed Fatback bikes with their extra wide wheels made easy work of the snow and ice, hundreds of twinkly little red lights disappeared up ahead. The cyclists far outnumbered the runners and the skiers.

One group that did confuse me was the Kick Sleds. These sleds are like prams on skies, the sort of thing you see huskies pulling, only the athlete pushes and rides the thing. Watching them riding the thing downhill made me wish I had thought of it. After all, they expended a lot less energy riding, even on the flat, they scooted along with one foot on the ski and the other propelling the thing forward, much like a child on a scooter (note to self, must have a go on one).

Another thing that I had noticed about this race was how very serious everyone was. I have raced a lot of Ultra distance races over the years and all over the world, the one thing that they all have in common is the esprit de corps, the 'all for one and one for all attitude- the mutual respect that comes from simply knowing that we are all struggling and suffering, basically the 'we are in it together' attitude. This was the first race that I had done when so many athletes passed by without so much as a "Hello, how you doing?" etc, just serious, head down, balls to the wall, competitive racing.

During the many races I have taken part in, I have been overtaken by just about every nationality and have always received a quick "Bonjour, wie gehts, come stai, como van las cosas" and even the Aussies manage a "Good day, sport," or whatever other language happens to pass by. The Americans, I'm sure, were so impressed by my athletic prowess that I had rendered them speechless!

One of the bits of advice I always give to any would-be Ultra Distance racer is do your own thing, go at your pace and no one else's. Don't, whatever you do, get carried away early on in the race. The adrenalin, excitement and fear of being last usually means that you start off way too quickly and end up paying a hefty price. Certainly with racing in sub-zero temperatures, the knack is to do everything slower. Going too fast early on is plain stupid and yet, here I was being bloody stupid and again I found myself going too bloody fast early on because of the fear of being last. (Bloody ego)

Up ahead, I could see two racers who seemed to be either competing against each other, or working together like cyclists do: one takes the lead for a while and then the other takes over, sort of drafting. I kept an eye on them, and they on me. Every time I looked up, they seemed to be looking back at me. This was the incentive I needed and, as usual, I adopted my now familiar race strategy of keeping the racer ahead in view, not letting them out of my sight and let them drag me along. They set the pace and all I had to do was follow, however, on this occasion, they were moving bloody fast and I was struggling to keep up – hence the fact that I was now sweating and the one thing you should always avoid in these conditions is sweating.

The trail was one of the best I had ever been on, well-defined, wide, hard-packed and straight. Looking up ahead, gauging my progress against the two runners ahead, I noticed that they had disappeared, and as the trail was so straight and clear, I couldn't work out how they had suddenly managed to sprint off so bloody quickly. It was only after a couple of minutes that I realised that there was a turnoff to the left. As I reached the turnoff, I spotted the two runners having a quick break. I pulled up, trying desperately to look cool and relaxed, but I somehow expect that my red, sweaty face and heavy breathing may have given the game away. As I drew level I said "Good morning," whilst pouring myself a coffee from the small flask that I carried on my hip belt. The two racers I had been following introduced themselves. Mike and Paul were brothers, they explained that this was the 9 mile mark. They then proceeded to ask whether I had ever done these sorts of races before and explained that the Arrowhead was a toughie. After a quick coffee, we left together and they then went on to tell me that they had both done the race before and were attempting the Arrowhead a Trois – this was an award given to anyone who had completed the Arrowhead three times in three years and using each of the three disciplines: cycling, skiing and running. One of them had skied and cycled and was now hoping that this would be his last attempt and the other had cycled it and his completion this year would mean he would only have to ski it next year before he received the much sought-after Arrowhead a Trois Trophy. This Trophy had only ever been awarded five times previously.

With such experienced Arrowhead veterans, I decided to pick their brains about the route and trail conditions. We had apparently done the easy bit and now the route would get progressively harder. After about twenty minutes or so, they started to pull away, keen, it would seem to drop the bumbling Brit. I let them go, envious of their impressive turn of speed, however, I would still try to keep them in sight if only because I knew that it was annoying them and, as my wife can testify, I can, at times, be bloody annoying!

Try was the operative word, they had obviously spent those few minutes at the checkpoint working me out and eyeing me up and realised that they had nothing to worry about, so they accelerated and left me standing.

Once they were out of sight, I did the sensible thing and slowed myself down and adopted a far more sensible pace. Plodding along at a more sedate pace, I felt a lot more comfortable. Occasionally, I would get overtaken by a bike or kick sledder and by late afternoon I had finally achieved my comfortable and familiar race pace. It seemed to get dark quickly, but because I wasn't wearing a watch, I hadn't got a clue what the time was. However, I spotted the checkpoint 'This way' sign with an arrow pointing to the right. About a mile later and I was there. The checkpoint was packed. It was a small shop that was attached to the side of a petrol station. Runners, skiers and bikers were sprawled in various states of undress all over the place. Bits of kit, bike helmets, ski poles and first aid kits were spread out every where. With just 35 miles done, it was surprising how many people had needed medical attention, blisters being patched up, cold weather injuries like frostbite and frostnip. The trouble with this checkpoint was that it was nice and warm, with really helpful and friendly supporters who offered not only hot food, but the chance to dry any wet/damp clothes. I accepted both gratefully.

I was keen to get moving. My back was sore and uncomfortable and would no doubt start giving me grief if I stayed nice and warm and comfortable. This getting too comfortable at the checkpoint had already claimed a few unsuspecting victims who had, for whatever reason, decided that enough was enough. A lot of people pulled out at this checkpoint.

I have raced hundreds upon hundreds of miles in Arctic conditions and I just couldn't work out why so many people were dropping so early on. Yes, it was cold but that is the nature of the beast, the conditions were as good as I could have hoped for: not many hills, no blizzards or whiteouts, the temperature hadn't dipped to any unmanageable levels, the trail was good, hard-packed and well-defined. The only thing that I could think of was the fact that the checkpoint was nice and warm, well stocked and friendly and was just too inviting and, as I was collecting my bits and pieces, prising my knackered old carcass out of the chair, I could see their point – who in their right mind would want to go back out into the dark, freezing night? Fortunately, I'm not in my right mind, anything but, and the simple fact was, I was more comfortable and far happier on the trail than I was in a checkpoint.

I left the checkpoint and had to locate and untangle my sled from the numerous bikes and sleds that had been discarded by athletes too tired or too desperate to get inside. Once I sorted myself out and found the trail I could relax, athletes cocooned in bulky cold weather gear, faces invisible behind the head-torches moved quietly towards me, heading for the checkpoint. After about 20 minutes, I reached the turnoff and peace and solitude returned.

For some reason, I always prefer to be on my own during these races. I'm quite happy pondering the meaning of life, losing myself in deep thought about nothing in particular, asking important questions like, who decided that deep frying a Mars bar would be a good idea? Why didn't Jimmy Greaves play in the 1966 World Cup Final and how much one of those Fatback Bikes would cost, anything and every thing has been mulled over during these races. It helps that I have a great imagination, without a great imagination this sport would be very difficult- trudging for hours upon hours with nothing to occupy your brain would be like poor old Sisyphus,* doomed to roll his boulder up the hill for all eternity: boring and monotonous, a thankless, seemingly-endless task.

*Sisyphus: Greek Mythology: King Sisyphus was made to roll a huge boulder up a steep hill. Before he could reach the top, however, the massive stone would always roll back down, forcing him to begin again and again.

I plodded along, trying to remember what it was exactly that Sisyphus had done to piss off Zeus, when I spotted the sign that announced that Elephant Lake was 40 km away. A little over 40km until the next checkpoint.

It was now very noticeable how few athletes were about, the field was at last starting to spread out. I like it like that, if only for the reason that the pressure was off, pressure to not get caught or pressure to not chase someone. A couple of cyclist came past, which surprised me, as I naturally assumed that all the cyclists would be far ahead. I could only assume that they had taken an extended break at the checkpoint, or had been somehow suffering some unknown problem or other.

It was now late in the evening and it was getting noticeably colder. The trail remained pretty good and not too challenging, consequently, I was able to maintain a reasonable pace, stopping for a quick coffee, some snacks and a warm jacket. I decided to use my iPod music thingy, though I had carried this little thing (it was about the size of a postage stamp) on my last big race the 6633 Ultra, I had been unable to use it – rules are rules and all that. After faffing about with the thing, I managed to switch it on without having to unpack, and put my glasses on. It was a revelation, why hadn't I thought of using one before? The music helped tremendously, or would have helped had it not been for the sudden and very unexpected Cliff Richard, singing 'Devil Woman' followed by Charles Aznovour singing "She!"

I blame my wife, me being the family Luddite, I had asked her to just download (that means put music on the thing, I think!) some music onto it. I must have been in the doghouse when the request was made because, Elvis, Dean Martin and Barry bloody Manilow also made an unwelcome appearance – that will teach me!

Walking along whilst trying to think who it was that sang "Shaddup Your Face", the beam from my head-torch suddenly started swinging from side to side. That's all I needed, a broken head-torch. Though not a problem, it was annoying, I would have to stop and bugger about to replace it with my spare. In these frozen conditions, stopping for any length of time is a pain quite literally: you start to get extremely cold extremely quickly and it usually takes me a couple of hard hours to warm up again. I was busy working out the logistics of my impending stop when a cyclist came past – it was his bloody lights that had been swinging from side to side. Panic over, I resumed my now familiar auto-plod.

Once the cyclist had passed, I was again on my own, listening to music and fending off the sleep monster. Occasionally I would catch sight of one of the trail shelters, these shelters were like bus shelters, a simple design, a roof and three walls, not comfortable enough to tempt me in, but reassuring enough to know that they were there should anything untoward happen. It was bloody cold and I had to pull my buff up and over my now freezing nose, like an armed robber. The trouble with using the buff to fend off the cold was the simple fact that it froze, froze solid – it was now like a ceramic face mask: it wouldn't move, no matter how I tried, I couldn't shove my much-needed Rolos into my mouth, I couldn't lift the thing up and I couldn't move the thing down. The situation was serious, I needed my Rolos. Now I could appreciate what a chainsmoker must go through every time they board an aircraft. I had to think of something, and fast. I took off one glove, grabbed hold of the buff and scrunched it, the resulting dent allowing me just enough room to shove 4, yes 4, Rolos into my gob. The situation was desperate, I had one shot at getting it right. Using just fingers and thumb wasn't getting the job done fast enough, so I made full use of the palm of my hand and shoved them all in. Once the chocolate had had a chance to semi-thaw, I entered the nearly orgasmic world of a chocolate extravagance: the heavenly pleasure of warm chocolate and toffee, waking up my underused tastebuds. The trouble was that my mouth was now so full of the chocolate toffee mixture that I was having to work hard at breathing through my nose, which was, alas, crammed full of the frozen nasal hair, hair that we men of a certain age are prone to. It felt like I was suffocating. Glove back on and gasping for breath in between desperate chews, I plodded on, thinking I really hope that I don't suffocate – 'death by chocolate'.

My back was stiffening up and now an occasional sharp pain in my right knee reminded me to be careful, slow down – I'm not as young as I used to be.

A while later, the trees disappeared and the whole trail opened up. It took a moment to realise that I was now on a lake. Elephant Lake was close to the next checkpoint at the Melgeorges Lake

Resort. Stepping onto the very exposed lake, the temperature seemed to drop, I could feel cold on my nose and face, the familiar sensation of frosting eyelashes and numbing nose and chin. I pulled my neck buff up but, unfortunately, it had also frozen solid. It was, once again, like a ceramic ring, this 2cm thick ring was not big enough to cover up both my chin and nose and, being rather fond of my nose or just plain vain, I chose to protect my hooter. With temperatures now somewhere between − 35/40C with a slight breeze, I had to try to speed up, lest I get frostbite again and then my wife would tell me off and might decide to stop me faffing about in these cold weather races. It was one of those do I stop and faff about and get organised? Or do I just carry on? Being so close to the checkpoint, I opted for the latter, knowing that the checkpoint was on the shoreline of this lake.

As I was plodded along, I was having to concentrate on the rapidly-disappearing route, the breeze wasn't particularly strong but being so exposed, it blew fresh dry powder snow onto what had once been a well defined path. Route markers were few and far between, so I became hyper-vigilant. I really didn't want to miss the checkpoint, I had done that once before and nearly ended up crying, the dilemma being that if you missed the checkpoint then decided to say "Sod it I'm not going to backtrack and look for the thing and add on the extra miles" you will be disqualified − you must hit the checkpoint.

As I approached the shoreline, I could see where the path meandered up towards a large timber building. Once I arrived, I was a little surprised that there were no sledges or bikes, nothing to indicate that racers were about. Luckily for me, someone spotted me and came over, explaining that the checkpoint was about half a mile away and pointed me in the right direction. Following the path led me to a huge log cabin and the reassuring sight of dozens of bikes and sledges. I grabbed various items − bits of food, flask, toiletries and first aid kit and made my way to the entrance.

I opened the door and was disappointed because it was warm,

welcoming, cosy, smelt inviting and had great big comfortable sofas, chairs and even some rather tempting beds. Some people had reserved small log cabins with showers, others were eating toasted cheese sandwiches and soup.

My lower back was giving me a bit of grief and I knew that I needed to rest it from pulling a sledge and, being in such a wonderful, comfortable checkpoint, would require an enormous effort to haul my carcass back out into the cold and I was also well aware that soon after leaving this checkpoint, the hard work would begin, with many hills, the route description had called these rugged, rolling hills.

As I stepped over and picked my way through the numerous bodies that were all in various states of undress, some eating, some sleeping, some administrating first aid and some were just staring into space, trying, I guess, to make the decision as to whether to carry on or not and, if so, when?

I found a small spot on the bottom of the stairs and, just as I was in the process of sorting myself out, I spotted Andy, another British racer. There were just three of us from Britain and Andy and his wife Jane were both cycling. I went over to speak to him and I couldn't help but notice that he had somehow managed to wangle one of the better chairs, not only that, it had a matching footstool which, I might add. he was making full use of. I asked whether Jane was there. He surprised me by saying that she had already left and worse, his race was over, due to frostbite on five of his toes! I was gutted for him, I've had frostbite and I know how painful it is. He explained that he was now just waiting to get a lift out. We carried on chatting for a few minutes when, suddenly, he was summoned – his lift had arrived. As we bade our farewells and, never being one to look a gift horse in the mouth, I grabbed his rather luxurious chair footstool combination. As I sat surveying the carnage around me, I decided to check on my own feet. Luckily they were okay: no blisters and, more importantly, no sign of either frostnip or frostbite. I was very conscious of the fact that, because I had had frostbite before, the one thing that I could not allow to happen was to refreeze my feet. I had got away with it once, to do it again would be both irresponsible and bloody dangerous.

Happy with the state of my feet, I decided to get some food, 5 bean soup and a cheesy toastie. I decided that this was indeed a great checkpoint: warm, comfortable, wonderful helpers, great food and a comfortable chair, OH NO – Comfortable Checkpoint Syndrome. I had already been here longer than I had planned, one more cheese toastie and I really must be on my way. Sitting in the world's most comfortable chair didn't help my back, it started to feel tight and, like a very old man, I slowly prised myself away from the thing and was glad when someone asked if I had finished with it.

I collected my bits and pieces, filled my flasks and stepped out into the frigid, cold, morning air. After faffing about with my sledge and holding back just long enough to watch the female athlete in front leave, I did this, not for any reason of chivalry or sportsmanship. I just wanted to see which way I had to go, once I was satisfied that she had got it right, I moved off.

It's always a bit of an effort after a long break, so I had no choice but to proceed slowly, after an hour or so, I had warmed up It didn't take long to realise that this section of the race was a little different to the previous seventy-odd miles: small, little climbs, nothing too challenging but they were a gentle reminder of the hills to come. Then the first of the nasty hills. Not particularly long but short and steep, steep enough for the two cyclists ahead to dismount. I did my usual head down. Small steps and liberal use of the poles, it didn't long before my poor old back started to complain. It was now that I made good use of the skill that had developed through my participation in so many other races, the simple technique of breathing through my arse whilst clambering up some horrendously steep hill. It worked and, in no time at all, I was cresting the summit. However, the elation was short-lived because, looming ahead was another equally steep hill. Same technique: head down and small steps. This part of the trail was a little more enclosed and, occasionally, a cyclist would come past which, at this late stage in the race, still surprised me.

It was now late afternoon, early evening. I pulled over for a quick sort-out. I needed a wee, something to eat and to get myself ready for the night section. Even though I had only stopped for about five minutes, the effort required to get moving and get warm was enormous and ,for the first time, I was glad that I had another little hill to clamber up.

Once on the top, I saw up ahead and to my left, one of those emergency shelter and, just in the front of it, someone had parked their sledge and was now sleeping on top of it. My inquisitiveness must have woken them up as a head popped out and asked me what the time was. Unfortunately, owing to the fact that I was not wearing a watch, I couldn't tell her. I asked if she was ok, she replied that she was but just tired. I moved off and realised that I had been awake for 40/45 hours, with just a catnap or two. Luckily, so far, I felt fine but I knew from past experience that it wouldn't be long before the sleep monster set up an ambush and pounced. I dug out my iPod and, even though it had said the battery was low, I decided that every little helped.

I was trying to remember what the next checkpoint was called, Ski Pulk. This checkpoint was the most basic: really just a couple of tents with water. Basic as it may be, I treated it as I always treat a checkpoint, – it was a stepping stone, another target to reach, another few miles closer. I focused on trying to reach the thing as quickly as I could. The terrain was not helping, with small hills breaking up any chance of a steady, rhythmic pace and then, suddenly, it happened. The familiar weaving started, like the proverbial drunk staggering home from the pub. I was weaving from one side to the other and it was only the fact that my trekking pole disappeared up to the halfway mark that woke me up and then my iPod died. I took a quick look behind to see if any one had noticed,- they hadn't, no one was there. It was time for one of my standing 30 second kips, with poles firmly planted in the snow, lean forward. Poles and body make an "A" shape, drop head, close eyes and nap, the beauty of this technique was that it had been honed and finely-tuned over many, many hundreds of similar miles. It had the advantage of resting the tired eyes, whilst not allowing for a deep sleep, simply because of the fact that if I fell asleep I also fell over. Having said that, I did once fall asleep during the Yukon Arctic Ultra, whilst standing, on that occasion I was apparently asleep for about six hours. Also, if anyone came up behind me, all they would see is some poor old bloke leaning on his walking poles who would appear to be either crying or puking The trouble with this technique was that it was just a short term problem solver, it was just delaying the inevitable, consequently, my 30 second catnaps would need to be repeated often.

I leapfrogged my way along the trail, having a quick 30-second nap roughly every 20 minutes or so, through tree-lined avenues and small hills. It was now late evening and I guessed that I had left the last checkpoint some 12 hours ago. I was now trying to work out the distance between the last checkpoint and the next, which I decided was about 40 miles. I was just in the middle of doing some rather complicated mathematical problem-solving equations, along the lines of how much bloody longer to the next checkpoint, when a fast-moving headlight beam came up behind me. A cheery female voice asked how I was doing. I lied, as usual and said I was feeling good. She then shot off – it took me a moment to realise that the voice belonged to the girl who I had earlier seen sleeping on her sledge.

Now I was thinking, should I have a proper kip? Hers seemed to have done her the world of good: no, plod on, if it was only 40 miles to the next checkpoint, I may well be only two or three hours away.

Occasionally, the trees gave way to wide, open spaces but these were short-lived and it was then back into the trees. Turning one corner and straining to see what lay ahead, I thought that I saw a light, but when I've been this tired before, I've seen elephants, dancing girls, groups of people drinking beer and motorbikes. I had learned to ignore such sightings. I carried on and then the light appeared again, only this time I thought I saw someone moving – bright light and slow-moving smoke made the whole thing reminiscent of the scene in 'Close Encounters of the Third Kind, when the aliens appear from the spaceship. Bloody hell, now I can add aliens onto the list of things seen when knackered. I carried on, pretending that there was nothing there, when a voice suddenly said, "Well done, buddy, you made it." I had indeed made it to the Ski Pulk checkpoint.

This checkpoint was a pleasant surprise: there were two small, heated tents and a lean-to gazebo-type thing. I had, for some reason, got it into my head that there would be just one or two small tents and some water (I wasn't even sure whether the water would be hot) and nothing else. I put my assumption down to either being bored with the pre-race waffle or just not listening.

The moment that I arrived, the support crew were brilliant, immediately asking me if I needed anything whilst at the same time guiding me into one of the two tents. It was small, empty and very warm. I sat down next to the stove, removed my gloves and hat and dried them in front of the stove. Hot chocolate arrived, I was in heaven, nice and warm, sitting down and after my second cup of hot chocolate, I decided it was time to move. That lovely, horrible feeling of getting comfortable, warm and relaxed was creeping up on me, trying its best to convince me to stay just a little bit longer. I compromised and moved outside and grabbed one of the chairs in front of the wonderful bonfire.

This was, I decided, as good as it gets – the whole area was a winter wonderland: beautiful, freezing, snow-covered tranquillity, a lovely warm mesmerising log fire with the hypnotic dancing, orange, crackling flames, another cup of hot chocolate and a seat. I savoured the moment and it was only with the greatest reluctance that I prised my carcass out of the seat and packed up, ready for the off.

As I was about to leave, one of the race crew informed me that there was just one nasty climb about five miles away and I only had about 26 miles to go. I thanked him and slowly made my way down the track -bollocks, I had thought that there was only about 24 miles left and I thought that there were no more hills. Why did I thank him? Note to self – start listening and paying attention to race briefings.

It wasn't long before I reached the 'nasty climb' and it really wasn't that bad, I had probably spent the last five miles or so worrying about the severity of the challenging climb ahead: it was a hill, but not the monster challenge that I had envisaged. Greatly relieved, I descended the other side and realising that I had just 20 miles or so left and it was getting light. I started to think that I might actually finish the race.

Though I was plodding along, trying to reach the finish line, thoughts of what next, what was going to be my next challenge? Unusually for me, I had nothing planned, I always have a race/ challenge lined up but, on this occasion. nothing. I needed another challenge, I was tired, my back hurt and I was still trying to reach the finish line of this race, and yet I was looking for another challenge. Had I become addicted to Ultra distance challenges?

I was just thinking about the tactics and techniques that I would need to employ to broach the subject with my wife, when I heard the unmistakable sound of a snowmobile. He slowed down and explained that the finish line at Fortune Bay was about 5 miles away.

I quickly had a celebration mouthful of Rolos and pushed on.

Coming off the trail, and onto what was now a proper road, buildings started to appear, as did people and vehicles. At last, I caught sight of a race marker, stating that the Arrowhead 135 finish was to my left. I had made it, turning off the road onto what appeared to be a driveway, I expected to see the overhead finishing banner and people clapping and cheering, but nothing. Just more trail I followed it, desperately scanning the area, listening and looking for any sign of the finish, nothing. I plodded on for another 20 minutes or so, before I finally caught glimpse of the finish line and the very welcome sight of the finish line banner.

The Arrowhead 135 is an odd race. The attrition rate is high, very high. During my race, there was a 35% finishing rate, the year before was worse: with 126 starters (all racers), only 38 managed to finish. Why??

The terrain wasn't particularly tough, both my previous Cold Weather races ie: the Yukon Arctic Ultra and the 6633 Ultra have tougher terrain and are far colder. Though I had struggled during the race, I put that down to a couple of things: one, having knackered my poor old back before I started and two, lack of sleep. Normally on races of this type, I would grab a couple of hours' sleep. During the first 30 to 40 hours, this race, with its 60 hour cutoff tempted me to keep going.

Arrowhead is a great little race, I would recommend it, but I'm still just a little confused as to why it's so bloody tough!

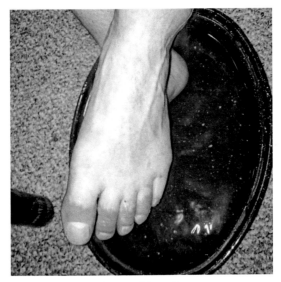

Andy's poor old tootsies

A relieved slightly knackered finisher

Just plodding along

The End

Chapter 3
Caesar's Camp Endurance Run

What is it?
A 100 mile trail run

When?
October

Where?
Aldershot, England

Distance:
30miles, 50miles or 100 miles (48km, 80km or 161km)

It is:
Brutal, 1520ft of climbing per lap (15200 for the 100, the terrain is in parts "Downright Brutal" – one of the toughest 100s out there).

See:
www.caesarscampenduranceruns.co.uk

I had first attempted this race in 2011. I had a spare weekend, so I thought I'd pop along, do a 100 miler and pop back home.

How wrong I was. After years of racing Ultras, I thought I knew a thing a two about 100 milers. Caesar's Camp was about to teach me a lesson, a very painful lesson.

This quietly-unassuming little run is held every October at Aldershot, on Ministry of Defence training ground.

There are three distances to choose from – starting at midnight, the relatively short 30 miler, starting twelve hours earlier, the tough 50 and the even tougher 100 milers. I, of course, went for the difficult option of 100 miles.

What made this race a little different and, for me, interesting was the fact that it was looped. I had always taken part in Point-to-Point races. I had never raced a repeated, looped route.

This race consisted of 10 x 10 mile loops, with checkpoints at the start and at approximately 5 miles. Easy, peasy or so I thought.

As usual, my cockiness and bravado would, once again, drop me right in it.

This 100 miler would prove to be anything but easy, bloody peasy. I should have read the course notes or race reports, but no, my lackadaisical, somewhat cavalier attitude would ensure that I would suffer greatly, moan loads and generally feel sorry for myself throughout.

As I made my way over to yet another race briefing, I realised that this race briefing was a little different: no gentle words of encouragement, no comforting, sympathetic morale-lifting words of wisdom.

Henk the race organiser, is, it would be fair to say, a no-nonsense kind of guy. His opening line was to inform us that "The course is shit, the music at the checkpoint is shit and the weather forecast is shit." the next fifteen minutes or so were full of little tips, such as, if you spend more than twenty minutes sitting on your arse at a checkpoint, he will kick you out, raining or not, knackered or not and you don't have to wear a headlight during the hours of darkness, however, if you should trip or fall, resulting in a broken, neck, leg, arm or anything else, don't go running to him, moaning.

As the briefing drew to a close, he called one of the runners out – Dave. Like a lamb to the slaughter, Dave made his way to the front. Henk proceeded to explain to all of us that Dave was here attempting the 100 miler for the fourth time and that, each time previously, he had failed to finish. Henk also, much to everyone's amusement, including poor old Dave's,went on to explain that he probably wouldn't finish this time either, however all was not lost.

In recognition of Dave's tenacious spirit, he would like to present him with an award. 'The Arsehole of the Year Award.'

Prize-giving ceremonies over, it was time to make our way over to the start line. As we shuffled our way forward, the inexperienced or supremely confident amongst us made their way to the front. The less confident, or more sensible, dropped to the back of the pack. I was in the latter group, and still deciding which category I came under, less confident or more sensible when, suddenly, the 10 second countdown began.

I set off at what I considered to be a sensible pace, but the severity of the terrain caught me by surprise. It was inconsistent and challenging. It seemed to change from loose stones to wet mud, severe drops and to even more severe climbs, boggy one minute and then wooded, undulating slippery tracks the next. One of my abilities in big, long races is the ability to maintain a consistent pace. It might be a slow consistent pace, but it was a consistent pace Unfortunately, this terrain did not allow for any consistency whatsoever.

It was on lap 4 that I really began to suffer. My feet were in agony and were swelling at an alarming rate. I realised that the damage from the frostbite that I had suffered just a few months earlier was now warning me that they were still not completely healed and I needed to be gentle. After 6 laps, I realised that enough was enough. I had to admit defeat and have only my second DNF in fifteen years of racing.

It wasn't so much the pain that stopped me. I'm used to that, after all, pain is part and parcel of extreme ultra-distance racing but the possibility of long term and/or permanent damage was something that I felt just wasn't worth it – no race is.

"A vow is a fixed determination to do a thing" – Mahatma Gandhi.

However, I vowed then and there that, like Arnie. "I'll be back"

Fast-forward two years and not a lot had changed. Henk was still informing everyone that the course was shit, the music was shit and the weather was going to be shit. Dave was here again and still trying to finish.

Three, two, one and we were off – some of those at the front would have given Linford Christie a run for his money. My little group also went off quickly, me included and, unfortunately I hadn't realised that I was running too fast until half way up the first hill. It was the fact that I was now breathing out of my arse that gave me a clue. I hadn't covered a mile and I was gasping for air and going bright red with sheer effort. Thank God that there a few sensible souls who were sensible enough to stop trying to run, and had decided to walk instead.

Less than a mile in and I was reduced to walking on my way up. I hoped that there were not too many of these hills, then I remembered that there weren't many but they were nasty and the cumulative effect would be unforgiving.

Once the summit was reached, the trail levelled off. It as just long enough for each of us to get our breath back before starting a tricky, technical descent. This ascending and descending was the order of the day. A couple of the descents had the potential to be dangerous. The first lap was congested with runners having to form a queue, and one descent in particular required the use of hands – grabbing hold of anything that seemed remotely stable, the loose flint-like stones rolled away from beneath each runner. Even if you were lucky enough to control your own descent, the runners behind were dislodging large stones that would try to crash into the backs of unprotected legs and ankles. Once you had managed to reach the bottom, a short, flat section that, fortunately, gave the legs a little respite, before once again taking on the tough technical terrain.

I was struggling on fresh legs, God alone knows what I would be like after four or five laps, which in turn translates to about twelve hours of knackering running.

Following the other runners, who all seemed to be very comfortable and were going at a pace that seemed a little fast but, not having the balls to slow down, I just followed, sheep-like. So busy was I in trying to keep up, that I hadn't noticed the little group splitting up. It was only at the very last second that I noticed the reason for the sudden split: a cattlegrid. Bollocks. I now had to make a decision: over the bloody thing or around the bloody thing? Being a cowardly custard or, what I should really say, erring on the side of caution, I went round. I carried on and, before long, the first checkpoint appeared at 5 miles. It was, unfortunately, a little too soon to make any great use of it, though I did notice that the tables and chairs were tempting us in for a rest- food and nibbles, jelly babies, fruit slices and chocolates. I made a mental note that this checkpoint would be made full use of later on.

Leaving the checkpoint, we made our way through a wooded area, then down a tricky little path to what appeared to be a small private fishing lake. The terrain on the second half of the course was a lot different from the first: more woods, boggy, slippery paths that had been churned up by the many runners in front which would, in all likelihood, get more churned up as time went on.

Some people were already walking. However, I had decided that, if I could, I would certainly run the first couple of laps. So I managed to catch and pass half a dozen or so but, as per usual, blokes being blokes, it wasn't long before I was being overtaken by the ones I had just passed.

Through undulating wooded areas, over stiles and besides what appeared to be a main road, the lap was certainly not boring. That might well change after the umpteenth time.

Down some small hills, through more woods and then, suddenly, the sound of the promised 'shit music' of the checkpoint.

Dropping down into the large and hastily-created temporary car park, we negotiated our way around the numerous parked vehicles. When I say, we, I mean the group of three that were just ahead and me, that I had desperately been trying to keep up with and had been stalking for the last 5 or so miles. The group of ever-patient supporters applauded our arrival and as we entered the little checkpoint tent, we were handed drinks and compliments. The race support crew were so dazzled and impressed by our amazing speed that they actually informed us that we were going so fast that, if we kept it up, we were on for a world record. A compliment indeed and I'm sure my chest inadvertently puffed out a little. A smile appeared and my head got just a little bit bigger. It was only when I left the tent did I have time to translate what they had actually meant, and what they actually meant was that we were a bunch of twats who were going too bloody fast. My puffed-out chest and puffed out head then deflated in unison.

I left the checkpoint a little bit wiser and vowed to slow down. The first lap at 1 hour 45 or thereabouts was much, much too fast – why had I not got the balls to realise it? I was lucky in that the stupidly-fast pace had not resulted in me getting either damaged, knackered or injured.

At least now, the field of runners had spread out, this in turn meant that the pressure was off, pressure to either keep up or keep ahead. I could plod along at my own pace.

Another good thing about the lack of congestion was that I could pick my own route which, owing to the congested first lap, I had been unable to do. I had had to run in any available empty space.

Even though I now had the luxury of route choice, it didn't mean that I was going any faster. In fact, the opposite was true. Looking down at the steep descent, the one that had required the use of hands was interesting. Whereas on the first lap, this descent was so congested that you could only really see the runners in front and feel the presence of the runner behind, therefore you couldn't choose where to place your feet you just sort of got carried along and placed your faith in the person in front – safe in the knowledge that if they fell or slipped, they had obviously come across a piece of ground that needed to be avoided. Simple. Now, however, I had the luxury of time and choice and I chose caution. This manifested itself in the fact that I came down the bloody thing like a big girl's blouse, scared of hurting myself or worse: falling and looking silly. I grabbed hold of anything that seemed remotely stable and then gently lowered myself down, inch by inch, until a few feet from the bottom, where I let gravity help and speeded up to get some momentum for the faster flat bits.

I continued on making a conscious effort to maintain what I now considered to be a sensible pace, I caught a few people and a few people caught me.

Whilst I had my sensible head on, I tried to memorise not only the route, but where all the obstacles were, puddles, stiles, potholes, cattlegrids, etc. It would not be long before it would get dark and, if I was lucky, I might be able to do three laps in the daylight but, like every thing else in this race, it was designed to be difficult and, consequently, we would do most of the running in the dark. The 30 mile run actually starts at midnight. The darkness, the tricky terrain and fatigue could spell disaster

Skirting around one particular tricky puddle, I caught sight of someone having a wee and, me being one to always take any advantage, I speeded up and overtook him.

I carried on feeling pretty good, no aches, no pains. I still felt quite fresh but I decided to be sensible with my pacing and have a quick break at checkpoint 2. I remembered how tough this course was and the damage the repeated laps could do. If I was sensible and patient I might, just might, be able to finish this race. After all, this would be the last chance- this was the very last time that this race would ever be staged.

Carrying on whilst trying to do some complicated mathematical calculations, like if it took 1 hour 45 minutes for the first lap and I had a 15 minute break on my second lap and I had 26 hours to complete the race, I needed to average, oh bollocKs, it's that cattlegrid again. This time I'll go over, not around, and it seemed to be quicker. On getting to the other side, I wasn't sure if it was any quicker but it felt quicker. Now, where was I? If it took 1 hour, oh forget it and just keep moving.

I couldn't see anyone ahead and, on a couple of occasions a runner would come sauntering past, which I'm sure wasn't easy because, being an indecisive chicken, I was zig zagging my way down the slippery, wooded paths.

Eventually, I reached the clearing where the checkpoint was located. Though the seats looked tempting, I refrained. Making small talk whilst grabbing jelly babies, small Mars bars and Coca Cola, I left a couple of minutes after arriving.

Fifteen miles down, eight-five to go. Scoffing down sweeties like a naughty boy made me feel a little better. I carefully negotiated my way around the little fishing lake just in time to see another runner disappearing around the corner. This runner was now my incentive. I promised to keep him in sight. I tried to speed up a little and I actually managed it but it wasn't enough,: the runner had now disappeared.

I felt ok and carried on, still trying to catch sight of the runner ahead and failing miserably. Eventually, I reached a clearing and another cattlegrid. Over the other side and onto a path that was slightly climbing. This path led to an even steeper path with some rather challenging steps, they probably only measured about 60/65 centimetres but required a bit of effort. I'm quite tall, so any shortarses in the race would have a real climb on their hands, especially later on in the race with very tired legs. Once on the top of this path, there was a clearing and then a straightforward descent before having to turn left and onto a very technical descent. This was made all the more difficult by the fact that it had been raining and the small, narrow path was now a sodden mudslide that required the utmost caution.

As I negotiated my way down, I noticed some impressive skidmarks, indicating to me that someone had had a bit of a nightmare descent. Once on the bottom, it was a question of dodging the rather deep puddles, before getting onto a nice well-defined path and then up through some trees, before dropping down into the car park and then the checkpoint.

This time I decided to have a seat, something to eat and a cup of coffee. It was whilst scoffing down my rice pudding that I noticed a couple of other racers looking a little forlorn. I looked at their race numbers and they were both doing the 100 miler. It didn't bode well, two laps, just twenty miles into a 100 mile race and they were already looking beaten. I decided to leave ASAP, knowing that listening to negative, defeatist people has an osmosis-type effect, with negativity creeping into peoples' psyche. I still felt ok but was very aware that, with 80 miles still to go, I would also end up asking myself is it worth it? I have nothing to prove, it's getting dark, it might rain etc etc.

I left the checkpoint whilst eating jelly beans and chocolate. The now familiar route was already becoming boring, the monotony of the repeated laps left me with nothing to look forward to, nothing to occupy my imagination, I couldn't ask myself things like what is around the next bend? Or what's over that next hill, I wonder where the checkpoint is? I hope the terrain gets easier, nothing to occupy a bored mind except the negative thoughts that I had overheard at the last checkpoint.

I carried on, trying to catch sight of the runner ahead and trying to keep ahead of the runner behind. The only distraction was the fact that the route was now really churned-up with so many runners going over the sodden ground. The technical route was getting more technical, this was annoying but good as it at least gave me something to concentrate on and if it should rain, as was promised, my concentration would have to increase and now I'm hoping it rains.

Standing on top of yet another hill, working out how best to tackle the descent, I caught sight of a couple of runners up ahead and gave chase, failed miserably, but at least, the little chase gave me something to do.

Approaching the checkpoint, I decided to have a quick break, have a cup of sweet black coffee, some nuts and crisps, then bugger off. On arriving, I noticed that this checkpoint was starting to get busier, with three of the seats being occupied and a couple, who seemed to be running the race as a pair, standing and scoffing. Always one to take a tactical advantage, I changed my plan to a quick swig of Coca Cola, grab a couple of handfuls of food and leave, thereby overtaking five people in one hit.

Once through the woods, down to the fishing lake and out the other side, then I got caught by the couple who were running as a pair and then about a mile later by one of the runners who had occupied one of the chairs. The five I had overtaken was quickly reduced to just two and I'm sure that it was just a matter of time. That's what I get for being a smartarse – cheats never prosper and they had all had a longer break than I'd had. Will I ever learn? I seriously doubt it. 53 years old and with 18 years' worth of ultra-distance races behind me and I'm still making cockups. If I was going to learn, I would have learned by now.

I carried on trying to keep ahead of whoever was behind me. Slowly ticking off each of my own little markers – the gates, stiles, turnings, boggy bits, climbing bits and slippery bits. I crept steadily forward, feeling good, finally up through the woods, before the final descent into the car park and checkpoint.

Once my number had been recorded, I nipped into the small tent, grabbed a chair and some food. 3 laps, 30 miles done, just 70 to go. I felt ok. I was going to finish this race this time. I sat next to a young guy who was talking to his running partner and they both looked fed up and pissed off. One of the guys, the one sitting down. had obviously fallen and had, it would seem, lost his sense of humour. They were both discussing the need to continue and the gist of the conversation seemed to be that it wasn't worth it. They had done 3 laps and that was enough, there was no point in continuing, it was going to piss down later and they still had time to get to the hotel and have a drink and something to eat.

They had a point: a decent meal and a nice warm bed sounded very tempting and was obviously the sensible thing to do, but ultra-distance running and sensible are not the best bedfellows.

Why enter a 100 mile race only to bin it after 30 miles? If they had been injured, I could have understood it but they seemed fine, physically. They had obviously hit a bad patch and, before realising it, had somehow managed to talk each other into knocking it on the head.

But hey ho, not my problem. I left the checkpoint not feeling brilliant, nothing physical just a bit fed up, couldn't seem to get my arse in gear. Eating handfuls of chocolate-covered raisins, and bored with the repetitive nature of the race, I decided to walk for a bit.

After about a mile, I realised that my walking had turned into plodding. I eventually arrived at the second checkpoint, not so much as plodding. more like moping – not unlike a petulant child who has just been told that Father Christmas won't be coming. I grabbed a chair, a bowl of fruit salad, some sandwiches and a cup of coffee. I was fed up, cheesed off and I couldn't snap out of it. I needed a tea-break and, after about twenty minutes of feeling sorry for myself, I got up and sauntered off, only because I was starting to feel guilty about taking up valuable space. I left the checkpoint still unable to get my arse in gear and, consequently, I again adopted my now-familiar plodding motion.

I covered the next five miles in much the same way, morose and despondent, in fact I decided that if my wife was waiting at the next checkpoint, I would knock it on the head and go back to the hotel.

She wasn't: the car park was nearly empty. Some thoroughly dejected-looking runners were collecting kitbags and traipsing back to their own cars. I made my way over to the checkpoint, had my number checked and registered, grabbed something to eat and drink, and left.

Not only did I leave, I actually started to run- well, shuffle along, my shuffle being only very slightly faster than a plod, but it was progress.

Why, what had happened between my entering the nearly empty car park and my arriving at the checkpoint? Was it the look on the thoroughly dejected runners' faces? Was it the fact that my wife wasn't there to rescue me? I didn't know the answer, all I knew was that I had hit my own personal bad patch and had been fortunate to have survived, managed to snap out of it and do another lap.

I had walked the entire fourth lap and now had to somehow make up for it. I forced myself to run/shuffle the easier bits. There weren't many, so I had to take advantage whenever I could. I felt better and could now see the lights of other runners, crossing from right to left, left to right, were they ahead or behind? I couldn't work it out but it gave some much-needed mental stimulation – concentrating on avoiding the puddles and the other runners seemed to make time go just a little more quickly and, before long, I was again entering the second checkpoint. Another hot drink, some snacks and I was off. Keen to make the best use of my newfound enthusiasm. I moved quickly through the fishing lake area and, eventually, the cattlegrid and the start of the climbing. I was fortunate that I caught sight of a runner up ahead and, as usual, thought I would use him. I speeded up and tried to chase him down but seemed to make no headway. He managed to keep the same distance between us. Then I noticed that he started to walk. I now decided to run because if I ran further up the hill than he did, it would surely mean that I was gaining on him. The plan sort of worked only until he realised what the cheeky bastard behind was up to and, once he got to the top, looked around and shot off.

As I crested the summit, I looked ahead for any sign of the runner I had been chasing, but nothing: he had gone and my cheating ways had been rumbled! With no one ahead, I quickly resumed my own pace and, again, runners' lights appeared all over the place.

I couldn't be bothered to work out my position in the great scheme of things,:were they in front or behind, were they on their fourth, fifth or sixth lap? It was irrelevant to me, all I knew was that I was still going, which was more than could be said of a lot of the runners.

I again reached the sodden mudslide, carefully negotiated my way down and around the puddles, then another twenty minutes or so later, I reached the car park. The now virtually empty car park, at least two-thirds of the cars had disappeared and with them the much needed supporters. I reached the actual checkpoint tent and grabbed a chair. Five down, five to go, or halfway there.

Now that I had snapped out of my sulking, moping, feeling sorry for myself mood, I was feeling good and relatively strong. I kept the time at the checkpoint to a minimum, keen to capitalise on my newfound enthusiasm. Leaving in a better frame of mind, I was able to pick up the pace. Knowing the route helped, I worked out the bits that were that were easier to run in and the bits that required a more sedate, cautious approach. I caught sight of a couple of runners. However, my newfound pace wasn't so good that I could actually catch them.

I adopted my usual stalking technique and held onto to the sight of them for as long as I could but, as usual, the inevitable happened. They disappeared.

Arriving at my favourite checkpoint, I grabbed one of the empty chairs. A couple of the crew were nodding. Dick, the guy who was running it, came out and asked me if I needed anything. I asked for a coffee, which duly arrived. I drank it quickly, realising just in the nick of time that I was getting comfortable. Getting comfortable at checkpoints is an Ultra runner's biggest no-no. I've learned to get the hell out of any checkpoint the moment comfort sets in.

And so it was that I set off, still feeling relatively happy. I jogged along the bits that were easier to jog in and walked the other bits. It was whilst walking along, that I heard voices behind me. I resisted the urge to turn around, and was still fighting the urge when, all of a sudden, two happy, chatty runners came past. How the hell could they still be talking and seem so full of energy? We exchanged pleasantries, when they informed me that they were just doing the 30 miler and had only started at midnight.

I felt a little better and made a rather feeble effort to pick up the pace, run a few steps, walk a lot more. I wasn't sure whether my speed had increased or not, but the fact that I was still moving in the right direction filled me with a little hope.

I carried on with my running, walking pace. Over the cattlegrid and up the start of the nasty climb – this, I tried to work out, was at the 7 or 8 mile part of the 10 mile lap. The two chatty runners ahead had disappeared. I clambered on and over the steps that seemed to grow in size with each lap, the slight descent allowed me to sort of hobble faster and, as usual, my slightly faster hobbling didn't last long. On I went until I was in the final wooded section before dropping down into the car park.

Arriving at the checkpoint, I felt good and keen to go, So I grabbed some food and left, I knew my feeling good wouldn't last so I had to take full advantage of it while it lasted.

6 down 4 to go. I didn't know what the time was but guessed it was somewhere between 04:00 and 05:00, not that knowing the time made any difference. I couldn't have gone any faster. Shoving in handfuls of Haribos' Tangfastics, the super tanginess soon woke up my redundant tastebuds, making my eyes go funny like when biting a lemon, if nothing else the combination of tangy taste and surprise certainly woke me up and seemed to put a spring in my step.

I kept moving forward, munching my way through the addictive Haribos. Arriving at the checkpoint, I grabbed a chair, had a quick coffee, a Coke, a couple of small Mars bars and half a banana and left, surprised by the fact that my feeling good moment was still with me.

It was not long after I left that I felt the first spots of rain, the wind had picked up and within minutes the heavens had opened. Not just a good old British dow pour, oh no, a real torrential downpour. It rained hard and loud, potholes were filling before my eyes, the T-shirt and lightweight gilet I was wearing were hopelessly inadequate. I was drenched and so hard was the rain against my face that I could hardly see. Why is, I thought, the wind always blowing in the wrong direction? It's the same when I cycle to work, it's against me on the way in then against on the way home. I plodded on, trying to make for some trees up ahead but, when I reached them, I realised that they afforded no protection against the horizontal rain. I stood for a couple of minutes and immediately started to get cold.

Knowing that I was just two-and-a-half to three miles away from shelter and a change of clothes encouraged me to get my arse in gear, all be it my rather soggy arse, in gear and get moving.

As I plodded along, trying to wipe my running nose on the back of my hand, I realised that it was now starting to get light, which made avoiding the puddles a little easier. I don't know why I was bothering to avoid the puddles: my feet were sopping, as was everything else. I ran up the small hill just before the car park, slid down the other side like some drunken amateur snowboarder and then made my way over to the checkpoint quickly, got my number scanned and then disappeared to find my plastic kit-box that contained some dry clothing.

I found the box without too much trouble, the little storage tent/ gazebo had once been filled to overflowing with kitbags, boxes and packs. Now however, there were just half a dozen items left. Unfortunately, some arsehole had obviously thought my plastic storage box was designed to be used as a seat, sat on it and had broken the lid – it was fortunate for me that I had packed my spare clothing into a dry bag. The water bottles, Coke and food were wet but the clothing was dry. I quickly got changed, base layer, gloves, hat, dry socks and dry shoes. What a difference. I made my way over to the checkpoint, grabbed a hot coffee or two. Feeling refreshed, warm and dry, I left. Seven down three to go.

I could now see light at the end of the tunnel, just three laps but now I remembered that the time had been cut from previous years. The last time I had done this race, there was a 30 hour time limit, this year, however, that time was reduced to 28 hours. Working that out, I would have to finish by 4 o'clock. I wasn't sure of the time but knew instinctively that I would have to pull my finger out, get my arse in gear, shake a leg or stop faffing about.

The rain had stopped, I was dry and warm and daylight had returned. I felt good. No blisters, aches or pains: it was now just a question of being able to go quickly enough for the last 30 miles.

Moving along as quickly as I could, dodging the freshly-formed muddy puddles, I also realised that this would be the last chance I would have to do this race: it was, as we were informed by Henk, the last time that the race would ever be held, owing to the spiralling cost that the MOD (Ministry of Defence) were now demanding to use this land, which was a shame because this race has a great reputation for being a tough, demanding and challenging race.

With these thoughts in mind, I tried to speed up and it wasn't long before I reached the 5 mile check point. Time was now the enemy, I stayed just long enough for a drink and a handful of jelly beans. I still felt reasonable but the now soggy ground was making progress a little more difficult and a little more caution was required.

Skirting around the fishing lake, being bloody nosey and not concentrating, my left foot disappeared into a particularly boggy, soggy bit. Extricating the thing required a firm, loud, squelchy pull, I now had the pleasure of running along with one wet foot that was not only caked in crap but annoyingly squelched every time I put my foot down.

I tried to keep up the momentum, plodding along, it wasn't long before I was again in the woods that were just before the car park.

Dropping down into the car park, I once again made my way over to the check point. It was now midday, I had just under 4 hours to cover the last twenty miles. It was a tall ask. I quickly worked out that the last twenty miles would have to be done as quickly if not more quickly than the first twenty. It was at this point that I realised that time had run out and, though I knew that I could do the distance, I also knew that I could not do the distance in that time.

I informed the race crew that I would have to finish. They agreed that It would be extremely unlikely that I could go quickly enough and they confirmed as much by saying that, though my last three laps were my quickest, they weren't quick enough.

The Caesar's Camp Endurance Run was, without a shadow of a doubt, the hardest 100 mile race I have done, even harder than the 100 miles I once did on a treadmill. It was the uncompromising technical terrain that made it so challenging, but what a race!

Henk the race organiser

2013

Caesar's Camp 2, David Berridge 0.80 miles done and I had run out of time I had run out of time

NOW WHAT?

Chapter 4
The Siberian Ice Marathon

What is it?:
More of a brilliant experience than a Marathon.

When?:
The 1st of March 2015

Where?:
Lake Baikal, in Siberia.

Distance:
26.2 miles, 42 kms

It is:
A novel race and an amazing experience, beautiful and fascinating, extremely well-organised and thoroughly recommended.

See:
www.absolute-siberia.com

This Ice Marathon really captured my imagination, Siberia was another one of those places that I had really wanted to visit.

Siberia, the word alone conjures up images of Gulags , frozen tundra, tough, unforgiving hostile terrain, in other words Siberia had ticked all the right boxes, except, maybe the Gulag part.

The chance to run 26 miles across a frozen Lake Baikal was just too tempting, at 636 km 395 miles long and 79 km 49 miles wide, Lake Baikal is the largest freshwater lake on Earth, it was much too good an opportunity to miss.

Unfortunately, the race was held on the first weekend of March 2015 and I had not raced since the Arrowhead 135 in January 2014, some 13 months before.

Injury (a torn meniscus) had occurred during the Arrowhead 135 and had prevented me doing much, if any, running until 9 weeks before the actual Ice Marathon.

To make matters worse, the Wednesday before I was due to fly out, I suffered from the effects of smoke inhalation.

In my 'real life' and far away from the world of globetrotting Ultra distance runner, I'm a Prison Officer (but that's another story) and it was whilst at work that a rather disgruntled inmate decided to set the place on fire. It was, according to the Press, a major incident and involved us evacuating 88 pissed off inmates.

I, along with four other officers had spent some considerable time at our local hospital having God knows what sorts of tests done and long periods on oxygen.

My participation in the Ice Marathon, was doubtful, so I kept quiet about the up and coming 'Siberian Ice Marathon,'

On the flight to Irkutsk I suddenly became the annoying bloke with the even more annoying cough. I'm sure the guy sitting next to me thought I was a disease-ridden unhealthy bloke who was likely to keel over any moment or at the very least I should give up my 60 a day smoking habit!

I just about survived the flight long enough to meet the race organisers at the airport, there were runners and languages from all over the world. Once the race staff were happy we were all there, we departed to a variety of coaches and on to our hotel which was a five hour drive away. Lunch was wonderful but again I had lost my appetite and could not stomach anything. This is my 19th year of racing, 19 years of racing extreme races and yet I still lose my appetite.

After reaching the hotel, I resigned myself to expect only the bare essentials, after all, I reasoned, the race entry only cost 540 euros, we were in Russia and they weren't going to spoil us with lavish luxury items such as decent accommodation – how wrong was I, we could have been in any swanky Swiss ski resort, (not that I have been in a swanky ski resort) A couple of lovely modern 4 star hotels, set beside ski slopes, busy chairlifts transporting well-heeled skiers to the mountain top, so that skiers and snowboarders could make their impressive descents down the three graded slopes, all of which finished right outside the hotel entrance.

Back in the hotel, my roommate arrived. Ben, a fellow Brit who was studying in Russia, (he did tell me what he was studying but, as usual, I wasn't really listening, selfishly I was too focused on myself and my lack of proper preparation). What I mean by that is that I was nervous (for nervous read shitting myself!) about my ability to finish with so little training and preparation, which was not helped by the constant coughing.

Ben was taking part in his first ever marathon. Once introductions were made and important decisions made, like which bed was whose, I adopted the age old, first come first served principle and grabbed my chosen bed. We then made our way over to a rather cramped race briefing. Much was made of the poor weather and even poorer ice conditions.

I hadn't really heard much about this race until about a year ago and yet there were runners from all over the world. Koreans, Italians, Germans, the ubiquitous Japanese even had the 'Ice Marathon Running Team', with team kit and banners. We listened intently, trying to glean as much information as possible, however, the two languages that were officially used were English and Russian, various translators did their best to translate into the relevant language but, as usual, like Chinese whispers, things got lost in translation and when the same thing is translated for the sixth time or the same question is answered, translated, relayed and repeated my boredom threshold reached overload, so much so that even though the English version is more than adequate,

I've lost just enough interest that the rest of the information becomes just meaningless 'white noise,' my feeble attempts at stifling yawns fooled no one.

Once the briefing was over, it was time for the evening meal. Unfortunately, my body's recurring habit of losing its appetite prior to a race was once again dictating the need to forgo the meal. Consequently, I decided to sneak back to my room and nibble away on my secret stash of goodies.

The following morning, after a rather unpleasant nights sleep, sleep that was constantly interrupted, thanks to my continued bouts of coughing, annoying and frustrating for me, but it must have been so much worse for my roommate, who had been unlucky enough to have drawn the short straw and got to share a room with a bloke that coughed all night, I felt really guilty, more so because it was Ben's first ever marathon. I'm sure that he must have thought about the act of murder, I know I would have! It's funny how I always seem to lose my appetite but I normally manage to sleep really well before any race, now, however I not only lost my appetite but I also lost a decent night's sleep.

I made my way down to breakfast and forced my self to eat something and drink copious amounts of coffee and fruit juice.

Onto the mini coaches for the 70 km scenic drive to the start which was along the shoreline of the great Lake Baikal, Lake Baikal itself was impressively imposing, huge in scale and with the gusting winds blowing powder snow along the icy surface, ice that was broken, jumbled, cracked and uneven, it was only now that I realised that this race was going to be a lot harder than I had realised. The coughing, congested lungs and lack of training were enough of a problem but now the weather and ice conditions would make the whole thing more daunting than difficult. I now began, for the first time, to wonder if I could actually finish this race!

Once off the coaches and onto the ice, the ice cold wind grabbed at you, trying, it seemed to find any weakness, any gap in the clothing that ,could be exploited and on top of that it was snowing.

Unfortunately, it happened that the icy blast was blowing the wrong way ie. straight from the direction we would be running. We would to all intense and purposes, be running headlong into a snow storm.

Coughing, limping and now freezing my rapidly diminishing nuts off, it didn't bode well, unfortunately my confidence was not high and what little there was, was rapidly disappearing. I needed all the help I could get so it was with a degree of desperation that I remembered the 'Sprinkling' Ceremony!

Lake Baikal is revered by the Russian people, and to the Mongolian Buryat people it is considered to be one of the most sacred places on earth. The 'Sprinkling Ceremony' was a chance for each of us runners to pay our respects and to show our reverence to this, the greatest of lakes. I'm not a particularly religious person, in fact, being a prison officer for over twenty years I have mastered the art of cynicism, however, things were now looking pretty desperate and I reasoned that desperate times called for desperate measures. I made my way over to where the small sprinkling ceremony was taking place, the language barrier was sort of overcome and I was offered a small glass of either milk or vodka. I erred on the side of caution and went for the milk, honest! Precise instructions were given, I placed my ring finger into the milk and then with a flicking action 'sprinkled' or flicked the milk onto the ice, this was done four times, one to each of the four compass points, North, South, East and West and then, lifting the glass to my lips and letting the milk touch them, I sprinkled the remaining milk onto the ice.

After the 'Sprinkling Ceremony' I wandered over to the hovercraft, these craft would be following us during the race, carrying race support crew, photographers and general race supporters and they were there as back up, rescue craft should the need arise.

Once I located my hovercraft (we were each allocated a numbered hovercraft) I handed over my 'drop bag'. These 'drop bags' were for warm clothing etc so we could get into something warm when we finished. I had planned to put in my superduper Arctic Expedition

Jacket and my pair of super warm Arctic trousers, however, when we were issued the bags, I realised that I would have to have a rethink: the bags were of an unfortunate size, they were just about big enough for a pair of gloves and maybe a hat, a very small hat and maybe just the one glove!

Once this was done, I made my way over to where I thought the start line was, this was somewhat difficult because the fast-falling snow was rapidly covering everything, the only clue to where the start line was, was that a group of people were huddled around together. As I trudged through the deep, soft snow I hoped they were on the start line, because if they were just a group of friends chatting, I'd feel a right pillock

As we stood around shivering and listening to the last minute instructions, instructions that contained ominous warnings about cracks in the ice and if the cracks were too big for us to skip or jump over they would be bridged with large wooden planks, we were to use the planks lest we fall through (or did he say 'follow through') and/or get wet feet. There would be no let up in the wind but it might stop snowing. The route, we were informed, was well marked with flags and every five km or so a marker board would indicate the distance covered and, as the countdown began, the more sensible runners started to appear, runners that had the good sense to take shelter behind the hovercrafts, toilets and even the supporters.

Two, one and we were off, as usual I tried to get a spot at the back end of the race. After the mass start free-for-all, we somehow morphed into a single file, which was good if only because the snow was deep and those in front of me were flattening the snow, thereby reducing the chance of snow getting into my shoes. Another good thing about the single file approach was that it prevented me from trying to being all macho and set off too quick.

Plodding along at a nice steady pace, following the heels in front of me oblivious to what was going on around me.

After about twenty minutes or so, the line got thinner and more spread out. Looking up ahead, I could see half a dozen of the 'racing snakes' pulling away, I envied their speed, but speed was not my main concern, it was the finishing. Could I really finish a marathon distance race in these conditions and with so little training

As the line got thinner and wider, I noticed a runner ahead carrying a flag – one of those promotional odd banana shaped things, I didn't envy him carrying a flag in these windy conditions, the flag would act more like a sail than an advertising hoarding. However, being a practical person (or just desperate) I figured that his flag-carrying during a Siberian snow storm would hamper him just enough for me to use him, use him as a pacemaker and for something to focus on. Happy with my dastardly decision, I plodded on, the snowing appeared to be lessening but the wind was still fairly strong.

Keeping the little red marker flags to my right I spotted the first 5 km marker board up ahead, however, the board actually said 7km, this was a little bit of surprisingly good news and cheered me up no end, 7 down just 35 to go!

The wind continued to blow hard but so did I, coughing and spluttering, I coughed up an unusually large chunk of something unpleasant, checking the coast was clear I spat it out. Unfortunately, I forgot that I was actually wearing a balaclava, the something unpleasant now became even more unpleasant when it was glued to my face mask. The good news was that it was cold enough to freeze in just a few short minutes which in turn made the removal of the frozen phlegm that much easier.

Approaching a checkpoint, I made a decision that was unusual for me during a marathon, I pulled over and made full use of the facilities, a couple of pieces of dried apricot, a handful of sultanas and a rather splendid cup of tea, it might have been lukewarm tepid tea and with no milk but it was, I decided, just perfect.

I would normally try and plod on nonstop but I was now trying to be sensible (a first for me), lack of training, nasty cough and not being entirely convinced about the supposed benefits of the sprinkling ceremony had me erring on the side of caution.

The good thing was that I could still see the flag-carrying runner up ahead, however, he did seem to be getting further away from me, maybe he had realised what I was up to.

I left the checkpoint, determined to keep him in sight for as long as possible, but soon realised that I wouldn't catch him, unless he was only doing the half marathon, with this eureka moment I changed my plan: I would keep him in sight until we reached the half-marathon finish line.

The snowing had virtually stopped and the gusty winds had now had a chance to clear the loose powder snow off the ice, which was diamond hard and crystal clear, like running along a marble floor. The Siberian Ice Marathon, was definitely a race that required the runner to wear some form of anti-slip device, the shoes I had chosen for this race were the Salomon Snowcross CS2. I had originally bought these shoes for the Arrowhead 135 but that race was a 135 miles long a consequence of which meant that I would be travelling very much slower, than I was now. When I took the Snowcross out for a test run just prior to the Arrowhead I realised that though they had great grip, they had shit insulation and even though the temperature was only hovering around the minus 20s my feet got cold whilst walking, however this Ice Marathon meant that I would be travelling faster and for a much shorter time ergo the Salomon Snowcross CS were far more suited to the shorter, faster race than the long, plodding race, plus the Salomon Snowcross had 9 in-built carbon metal cleats that were brilliant at gripping the marble-like ice. With such great traction came confidence, confidence in not slipping, but, unfortunately, not so confident about my being able to cover the 26.2 miles.

I carried on, still trying to work out the possibility of actually finishing the race, when I noticed up ahead a crowd had gathered and there were a couple of stationary hovercrafts. Had there been an accident? Had someone collapsed? Had someone gone through the ice? Had the hovercrafts broken down? It was only when I got nearer that I realised that it was the halfway mark or the half-marathon finish line.

Now I had a decision to make, I had been plodding my way forward far slower than I would normally 'run' a marathon, my legs and in particular my quads* felt as though they had been tenderised. I wasn't really moving fast enough to generate any warmth and the coughing fits weren't helping. Could I do another 13.1 miles on my rapidly-declining physical ability?

Watching the half-marathon finishers celebrating, hugging, high-fiving and getting dressed into warm clothing made the thought of stopping even more tempting

Continue or quit, I weighed up the pros and cons. Why should I quit? Yes, my legs hurt, however, they were still working and still carrying me forward, yes I was coughing, but I would be coughing even if I stopped and yes I was cold, but it's bloody Siberia! Those three things were just minor inconveniences – annoying and uncomfortable but no real reason to pull out of this once-in-a-lifetime race: man up, shut up, grow a pair and get on with it!

I left the half-marathon checkpoint, still not entirely convinced about my chances of finishing but one thing was clear – I would now give finishing my best shot.

I would attempt to run to the first couple of marker flags, see how I felt and then make a decision. I remembered a bit of advice that I was given years ago by an experienced Ultra runner and that was to never ever 'give up' whilst at a checkpoint.

It was shortly after leaving the checkpoint that I realised that it was once again starting to snow and the windspeed seemed to picking up, though, thankfully it was not blowing straight at me. It was, however, blowing across from side to side, one side of my face was getting cold and my bloody race bib was billowing like a bleeding sail trying to push me over to one side.

Another marker board and another hastily-constructed wooden bridge. It was now noticeable how spread out the field was. There must have been a lot of people in the half-marathon, the runner with the flag had disappeared.

*Quadriceps - the quadriceps femoris is a large group of muscles on the front of the thigh.

As I negotiated my way across the wooden bridge, a thought occurred to me, this is the first double digit run that I had done for over 14 months, the biggest distance I had run in a single run was a little over 8 miles, though I had been doing two small runs a day – no wonder my poor old legs were protesting.

Another thought occurred to me, I would, finish this marathon come what may, I even resigned myself to the fact that I might be last but I didn't care. I would finish, end of story! With that simple decision made, I could relax and concentrate on the simple act of putting one foot in front of the other until I reached the finish line.

Another little promise that I made to myself was that I would not walk: my shuffling, plodding forward locomotion was quite possibly slower than walking but it was working and sort of comfortable, I think.

With luck, I should make it. I just reduced the race down to bite-sized chunks, using the little red route marker flags, one flag at a time.

The weather was not playing fair, it was still trying to snow and the wind had not let up.

Plodding along in a my own little private world, I suddenly became aware of some very peculiar noises, strange acoustics that were intermittent and irregular all around, it was like listening to some 'tranquillity CD' of relaxing whale music, like whistling dolphins, then every so often there was whiplike crack and a thump. The trouble was that we were on a lake and the acoustics would seemingly echo off the surrounding landscape.

Lake ice, like all ice, is dynamic, constantly expanding and contracting, the resulting noise can be a little unnerving, however, I have travelled hundreds of miles over ice and I have heard some very unnerving, trouser-filling noises. These noises were anything but unnerving, it was different, pleasant even. Trying to pinpoint the exact location of the noise was impossible, it was like listening to surround sound, only the noise was not only all around but above and below. I gave up and just enjoyed the free show.

Every so often the super flat marble ice was broken and jumbled, chunks of broken ice pierced through the surface, like flotsam, bits and pieces floating on the surface. The loose bits of broken ice, trapped the blowing snow, which then collected, making small drifts, which in turn caused me to alter my pace and pick up my feet.

Though the snowing had ceased, the wind had not and because it was strong and gusty,and blowing from one side to the other it was a constant battle to not be blown across the ice. Approaching the 30 km, it was noticeable how much the wind had picked up.

The small red marker flags were not only able to show the way but also showed the wind strength and direction, which was now predominately from the left. Curiosity got the better of me and I turned my balaclavaed head into the wind and instantly regretted such a stupid move, not only did the sub-zero wind chill, slap and sting any exposed skin but I could see, heading towards us, a snow storm.

The natural topography of the lake meant that the surrounding hills had channelled the falling snow into a funnel-like tube, the approaching snow looked like white smoke, thick and rapidly approaching. For some strange reason, I momentarily thought about speeding up to try and outrun it but quickly realised the futility of such a stupid act. When the snowstorm did hit, it was mercifully short-lived and had looked far worse than it actually was. Lasting 15-20 minutes, it passed by and was instantly replaced by clear, calm weather. I plodded along and, to my right a hovercraft passed by, looking at it I noticed the shoreline behind it, it really was like being at sea and catching a glimpse of land ahoy. Now, for the first time, I thought that I would manage to finish.

The ice we were now running on was black, jet-black marble-hard ice, extremely slippery, so much so that I had to concentrate hard on making sure that I gripped the ice with each step. Once or twice my foot slipped, even though the carbon cleats had thus far performed well, the super-smooth, marble-hard black ice was challenging.

Not daring to look up too often, in case I fell, I suddenly became aware of a figure moving rapidly across my intended path – it was an ice skater. I was envious of the way they glided along, almost effortless, using a long, graceful gliding motion they covered a huge amount of ground quickly and easily.

We runners, on the other hand, were slipping and sliding and, with over 20 miles in our now knackered legs, must have looked ridiculous.

It was while enviously watching the oh-so-graceful skater that I caught sight of the far bank and what appeared to be buildings. I reasoned, more out of desperation than anything, that where there are buildings, there must be a finish line. A simple, desperate logic, by a simple and very desperate man. I kept my eye on the far bank, even trying a rather feeble effort at speeding up.

Within twenty minutes or so, I detected movement – people were moving, not running, just moving like normal people, milling about and chatting. Then I spotted a massive ice-carved sculpture, numerous Russian letters carved out of ice spelling out, I guessed, the name of the town. Passing the ice writing, I slowly approached a couple of well-wrapped people helping the rather pitiful marathon runners across a short section of wet, slushy ice. I was guided like a decrepit old man over the soggy planks that were being used as a makeshift bridge, once across it was just a couple of 100 metres before I crossed the finishing line. Time checked, I saw my roommate, Ben, waiting for me – not only was he waiting but he handed me a doughnut, it was worth the 26.2 miles for the doughnut which I gratefully took and scoffed with as much dignity as I could muster.

The 'Ice Marathon' was, I decided an amazing experience, and one that I would thoroughly recommend: well-organised, low key and stunningly beautiful and worth every penny. I was pleasantly surprised.

Photographs by Maria Shalneva

The Runner's Nuts

Chapter 5
The Gobi March

What is it?:
A multi-day stage, desert race.

When?:
May/June 2015

Where?:
The Gobi Desert, Xianging province, China

Distance:
250 kms (155 miles)

It is:
Fantastically challenging, varied and an experience to cherish.

See:
www.4deserts.com

The Gobi Desert is the fifth largest desert on earth. It is, as we found out, also a desert of extremes, extremely hot, extremely cold, extremely wet and extremely challenging which was, of course, obviously a good thing for an extreme race, such as the Gobi March.

Ironically, it was only after leaving the hotel in Hami, the largest city in the Xinjiang Province of the peoples republic of China that I could start to relax.

The journey to the race was right up there with any of my previous challenging adventures.

Starting with an e-mail from China Southern Airlines just five days before departure, 'Dear Mr Berridge, we regret to inform you that your flight to Hami has been cancelled'

Now, I am not, by nature, one of life's panickers, however, it was Saturday, things and places would be shut for the weekend. Consequently, I would have just two days to sort myself out some flights to an obscure and little-visited region of China, flights that had taken me weeks to sort out would now have to be redone in two days!

There followed 48 hours of frantic phone calls, e-mails and foul language, language that was sort of muttered under my breath (If only because, at this late stage, I could not afford to upset anyone who was in a position to help).

Fortunately, the flights were finally sorted, unfortunately, this incurred even more expense, expense that the ever-patient Mrs Berridge was not best pleased with. I knew I had some grovelling to do when I got back!

The flight was on Wednesday 27th May, I would be flying or hanging around airports until Friday, when, I was assured, the pickup to the race HQ would depart at 14.00 for the 10 hour drive to the Hami Hotel.

The 12 and a half hour flight to Guanzhou was uneventful, spoilt somewhat by the fact that, as a last minute passenger, I was given the only seat available, the toilet seat or, should I say, the seat right beside the toilet. The constant coming and going, the odorous aroma of upset stomachs and nervous fliers, made the whole last minute ad hoc, seating arrangement less than ideal, but, I reasoned that beggars could not really be choosers.

Glad to finally get off the plane, I had a 5 hour wait for the next flight to Urumgi, before finally arriving at Urumgi at a little after midnight. I was knackered but still had a fourteen hour wait until the bus that would be taking us Gobi March runners to the race start picked us up.

Owing to my already limited funds being so depleted, I figured that, rather than have the added expense of a hotel, I would kip at the airport for a couple of hours, thereby saving a bit of money which in turn would score me Brownie points* with Mrs Berridge and as my Brownie point piggybank was very nearly empty, I needed all the points that I could muster. Unfortunately, however, I had not taken into account the Chinese Airport Security, for no sooner had I found my chosen 'bed' for the night, tucked away nicely and out of harm's way, quiet and with a panoramic view, then the security team arrived and kicked out all the vagrant -looking types.

Luckily for me, the moment that I was ejected from the airport building I was ambushed by an enterprising, opportunistic taxi driver who spotted me, approached and asked if I needed a taxi, It was half past two in the morning, I had been awake and travelling for a little over 30 hours. Chinese Security had chased me out of the airport and I had nowhere to go. My defences were down, consequently, I had little or no choice. I asked him how much to take me to a hotel, I figured that this guy was the hunter who had now locked onto his cornered prey. It was now that he would pounce, and charge me a small fortune, because, like me, he also knew that I 'had little or no choice.' I braced myself, ready for the inevitable verbal sparring match that was about to commence. I was lucky, indeed, because he just happened to know of a hotel and it was 'A very good, special hotel." Then the bastard took the wind out of my sails by saying it would only be $5, five US dollars, to take me. I must have misheard him – $5 – a little over £3, this was to good to be true. I gave him the $5 plus another 3 making it clear that he had been paid, there will be no more.

I got into the back of the car, rather pleased with myself and my macho stance. It didn't last long: driving through deserted Chinese streets at half past two in the morning, my tired brain started to ponder on a worse case scenario. Was I now being taken to some back alley where his mates would be waiting to pounce, rob me, sell me into white slavery or murder me and then break me up for my body parts, body parts that would be sold on the lucrative black market? Just as I was trying to work out how much my kidneys would be worth and various ways of defending myself, we pulled up in the front of what looked like a half-decent hotel. I felt a right prat!

At 09.00, after a much-needed sleep, I was taken to the airport, by the hotel courtesy vehicle.

After grabbing a bit of breakfast, I sat people watching. Then I spotted someone who was also waiting for the Gobi March bus. We waited by the designated pickup spot and were joined by some other runners before finally departing for what would be a 10 hour drive to the hotel. I arrived at 23.15, was knackered. Introduced myself to my roommate, Riz and promptly fell asleep.

The next day was spent going through the laborious admin procedure, all the necessary documents, such as medicals, insurance and waivers, all the compulsory kit was checked, as was food and hydration requirements. My pack was weighed and was confirmed as being 8.5 kilos. Nearly half the weight of my room mate Riz's whose bag had weighed in at nearly 16 kilos.

Eight point five kilos was a world away from the 13 plus kilos of my very first race, the 1996 'Marathon Des Sables' (was I finally getting the hang of this Ultra running malarky?)

*Brownie Points: are a hypothetical social currency which can be acquired by doing good deeds or earning favour in the eyes of another.

But, being the smart arse that I am, I figured that I could get my pack down to less than 8, so started getting rid of kit that I would,, in all probability, not use. Bearing in mind that I had spent weeks collecting and selecting only essential things that would be NEEDED! So out went 4 hydration sachets, some coffee and chocolate sachets, fruit pastilles and high energy sports beans I also got rid of waterproof leggings and a buff. The pack didn't feel that much lighter but it made me feel better.

The following day, and it was all aboard the various coaches for the long drive through rural China, the convoy must have looked impressive with Police and security escorting us. 4x4 Gobi March race vehicles festooned with the Racing the Planet logo, looking to all, like mobile advertising hoardings.

After a couple of hours driving, one of the girls could wait no longer and asked if we could stop for a toilet break. Why is it I thought that girls can do that, blokes just sit and suffer in silence, girls ask – a bit like asking for directions: blokes would sooner get lost than ask, whereas girls would sooner ask than get lost. As soon as the one bus pulled over, the others followed, 164 runners and numerous race crew and staff all had the same thing in mind and so it was girls to the left and blokes to the right and with 50 or 60 blokes all peeing against a small wire fence, which was a great relief in more ways than one. Had the fence had been electric, well, 'nuff said. Back on the coach and on with the drive, the place was beautiful and green, not at all what I was expecting. We seemed to be climbing ever higher, the once smooth, asphalt roads were now transformed into rough narrow country tracks, turning right through some large rocks, we came across loads of people who appeared to be having a party.

The party turned out to be a welcoming party and we were the special guests. We stepped off the coaches and followed directions to a large cluster of what appeared to be green army tents, all the tents were numbered and we had all been allocated a tent, mine was tent number one!

The reception was amazing, we were clapped and cheered, music was being played by some local musicians, there was dancing.

I stepped in and my fellow tent-mates followed – two New Zealanders, Jo and Richard, father and son, Chris and Sam, husband and wife Simon and Katherine, Dave, an American, and Riz. The nine of us would become tent-mates for the next few days but, as I was one of the first ones in, I grabbed what I considered to a prime location – on the right by the door, that way I only had a person on one side of me (just in case of possible snorers) and near enough to the exit for me to sneak in and out for a wee without disturbing anyone.

Once I had got myself sorted, sleeping bag out, kit laid out etc, I wandered over to one of the many small campfires. There was a real party atmosphere with singing, dancing and music. We were made to feel incredibly welcome, some of the runners got up and danced, we mingled and introduced ourselves, usual race time talk of war stories about previous races.

As I looked around, taking in the stunning scenery I noticed, for the first time, that we were actually in a sort of depression surrounded on all sides by rocky outcrops and armed SWAT teams, who appeared to be strategically-placed on the high ground. I also noticed that we were actually penned in, the whole camp site was taped off and little groups of security guards were patrolling the perimeter. Were they there to keep us in or to keep others out, I wondered?

We were at an altitude of 2400 meters and it was bloody cold and there were ominous-looking dark clouds gathering. It looked as if it might actually rain, memories of my last desert race came flooding back, The Namib Desert Challenge, it pissed down. As is normally the way in the desert, once the sun dipped below the horizon, it was dark, very dark, very quickly.

We all sort of made our way back to our respective tents, it was too cold to faff about and to make things even colder the wind had picked up and seemed to be blowing straight into our tent. It was at this point that we noticed a flaw in the tent's design. The tent didn't have a zipper on the entrance way, it had velcro and, unfortunately, the tent was either too small or had been put up incorrectly because the two velcro strips were just too far away from each other to make full contact, like a rather buxom size 16 ample-bosomed lady trying to squeeze into a size 12 blouse; resulting in a lot of stretched fabric, a mighty effort was called for. Consequently, it took two of us to pull the two sides together and even then there was a gap at the bottom of about half a metre – the wind whistled through.

Because the tent had been pitched on a slight slope, I had to sleep with my head to the centre of the tent, otherwise my head would have been downhill, unfortunately this meant that I was now directly opposite the wind-tunnel, gap. Consequently, I had to use my rucksack to keep the wind off my face. Just as I got myself, sorted out some selfish git wanted to go out and use the toilet, opened the tent flap and the whole laborious process of sealing the gap started again and then it rained and, boy, did it rain. The flap was flapping, the rain was raining and I was freezing. It was, I decided, going to be a long night. It was a little after 04:30 that I was awoken by someone discretely farting which then seemed to start a chain reaction of coughing, farting and fidgeting.

Other tents seemed to be doing the same. The camp staff were lighting the fires and boiling water. I curled up and tried to go back to sleep, it was too early and too cold to get up, however, my bladder dictated otherwise.

After a quick wee, teeth clean and a cup of coffee, I started to pack my rucksack. It was bloody cold, too cold to sit in the tent, so half an hour or so prior to the start of the race, groups of runners could be seen, huddled around the numerous, small campfires.

The race briefing commenced, we were informed of what lay ahead, tricky technical bits to be aware of and weather conditions, which didn't sound encouraging. Oh, and apparently we had a sand dune to clamber over!

STAGE 1

The Sand Dune of Barkhol

Once again, I found myself standing on the start line of some epic adventure and, once again, I realised how very lucky I was. After twenty years of racing, I appreciate that I am healthy enough to be here, that I'm able to travel to some amazing parts of the world. I appreciate my wife and her acceptance/tolerance of my wanderlust. I'm lost in thought, when the group starts to shuffle forward.

Multi-coloured clad runners, every shape, size, age and nationality was represented. Some of the security guards formed what appeared to be a guard of honour. Three, two, one and we were off. Trying to run slowly whilst running down hill amongst the excited group was not easy, but I tried anyway. The natural topography of the place was stunning, lush and green with weirdly-shaped rock formations, though initially easy underfoot, it wasn't long before the overly-excited running group I was in, were suddenly reduced to carefully negotiating a way through what appeared to be a dried river bed. The less confident were annoyingly slow, the more confident, less patient of us took silly risks and ploughed on past. The terrain sort of levelled off and I could finally go at my own pace, checkpoint one appeared after about 6 km. A quick top-up of water, though I hadn't drunk that much but knew from experience to always grab the opportunity to keep water bottles topped up, just in case. I left the checkpoint feeling good, because I was, at last, warming up. Plodding along at my usual pace I spotted what I thought were snowflakes, quickly dismissing such a silly notion as completely ludicrous – snowflakes in the desert, whatever next!

I was joined by a well-wrapped-up German runner. Christian introduced himself and we plodded along together, chatting and generally passing the time. It was then that he mentioned that he thought it was trying to snow. Thank God, I hadn't got the guts to mention it lest it had been a figment of my overactive imagination. After we reached the second checkpoint, the support crew confirmed that it was indeed trying to snow.

Normally, I don't mind racing in the snow, I've even raced in the Arctic. The difference is that, one, I had chosen to race in the snow and two I was prepared to race in the snow – now, however, I had chosen to race in a desert and was only prepared to race in the desert.

Ah well, no point in moaning about it, even my moaning was not going to change the weather.

The snowfall increased as did the wind, unfortunately, it wasn't proper snow the sort you get in Arctic environments. Oh no, this was more like good old British snow, wet, when it made contact it, melted. The wind had picked up and that, combined with wet snow, increased the wind chill, which in turn meant that the warmth I had managed to generate was now gone, I was bleeding freezing. Christian, however, being the well-organised teutonic type, decided that it was now time to break out the poncho and what a poncho, big enough to cover both him and his rucksack and it even had a hood. I was impressed. I had slept in tents that were smaller. It was, I decided, the Rolls Royce of ponchos, mine on the other hand was more Reliant Robin than Rolls Royce, big and robust it was not, flimsy and disposable it most certainly was, I only bought it because it cost £1.99 and was on the compulsory kit list, I didn't think for one minute I would need a poncho in the desert.

We carried on, eventually reaching what appeared to be a small dam, crossing to the other side, we noticed a 4x4 Police vehicle watching us and waiting.

The snowing got worse, the wind increased and visibility was becoming limited. I was freezing and bitterly regretted being a smart arse and dumping my waterproof leggings back at the hotel and for not investing in a decent bloody poncho.

We ran and walked our way to the next checkpoint, which was by now covered in snow and the flimsy gazebo was only just about surviving the maelstrom.

The support crew in any race are the real heroes, without whom it would not be possible to put on a race. They are the backbone and now in these appalling conditions their true value could be appreciated. It was freezing cold, wet and windy they hung around waiting, and still they managed to smile, encourage and help us.

Once I was ready to leave the checkpoint I was given instructions by one of the crew who pointed in the direction of what he assured me was a sand dune and, as visibility was somewhat limited, I took his word and wandered off in the general direction that he had suggested.

It wasn't long before I reached an impressive-looking snowdrift, I could just about make out the small pink flags, that were leading me to the foot of the snowdrift. It was only when I started to crawl up the thing did I realise that the snowdrift was in fact a sand dune. The mythical Sand Dune of Barkhol, a sand dune covered in a thick blanket of snow is to my mind a snow drift.

It required an enormous amount of effort and I was now having to work hard: the dune was bloody steep and incredibly soft underfoot. My breathing became laboured. Once I reached what I hoped was the top, the marker flags went off to the left and then the real climbing could begin. Looking up ahead I could see nothing. Though the wind had blown up the side, that same wind was now blowing me from the left and trying to dislodge me. It took all my effort to not get blown off. It was, I realised, nothing less than a blizzard, I couldn't see ahead so focused on the footsteps in front, just one step at a time. I was still working hard, too hard, trying to climb a dune and retain my balance, the drops either side were severe and I knew without a shadow of doubt that if I got blown off to one side, which was a distinct possibility, I would not be physically capable of climbing back up. I'd probably end up crying and swearing at the foot of the dune.

I remembered that the Official Course notes had said the dune was a 1 km climb and even though I was breathing out of my arse, I was determined to climb the thing without stopping, no matter how slow. I would not stop for the whole 1000 metres. Unfortunately, that plan went out of the window, I needed a quick stop, just to slow my heart rate down, the combination of fear and effort had sent my heart rate racing through the roof.

The moment I stopped, I realised that someone was following close behind, which in turn meant my rest was cut short and forced me to get moving because there was absolutely no room for people to pass.

I plodded on, reached the top and never did see the summit. At some point, I realised I wasn't climbing any more. The descent was gradual and for the first time on the dune I saw someone ahead, then I noticed one of the race crew putting in or removing the marker flags, then a few more runners came into view. I was just trying to work out what was going on when I realised the runners had not gone over but had in fact gone around the dune. My immediate thought was that they were cheating bastards, it was only later that I discovered that the blizzard-like conditions, coupled with zero visibility had meant that the dune was deemed too dangerous to allow runners to attempt to climb it. Typical, I actually manage to get my arse in gear, clamber over a snow-covered sand dune, only to see slower runners catch me up and save a whole load of effort in the process, from cheating bastards to lucky bastards. Oh well. Que Sera, Sera. A mouthful of Haribos, a quick drink and I was once again a happy bunny. (It doesn't take much!)

The terrain seemed to be more user-friendly, it was still snowing but nowhere near as much as it had been. Looking around, we seemed to be entering a more cultivated area, small fences appeared and clambering over and around a few, the ground had a distinctly agricultural look about it. Crossing what appeared to be fields, the snow was now trying to stop, leaving the ground wet and muddy. In the distance, I spotted what looked like a main road. It was probably a couple of km away but between me and the road was a large muddy field with a slight incline, the mud was slippery and my training shoes afforded absolute zero traction. I was trying to slide my way uphill which was annoyingly frustrating.

As I inched my way forward, I could see a couple of the Racing the Planet race vehicles. When I finally extricated myself from the quagmire-like field, I was given directions and told the finish line was just 2 km away.

Following the directions given, I plodded along and then a couple of runners caught me, one of which was Sam from my tent, he looked annoyingly fresh.

The route taken was through a small underpass and then the wonderful sight of the finish line. This campsite was called Yurt Village, with numerous yurts* dotted about the place. I was asked what my tent number was and then informed that the biggest, grandest Yurt of all was to be my home for the night.

*Yurt

A yurt is a traditional portable round tent, used by Mongolian Nomads. It is usually covered in either skins or felt.

I made my way over to the yurt that could only be described as Le grande Marquee, the outside looked huge, the inside looked spectacular: large and spacious with a fully-fitted carpet, light and airy with a small gas heater. With just three other runners, I virtually had the pick of my sleeping area. I was looking forward to a decent night's sleep.

Rucksack off, shoes off, I stepped in, eager to secure my place. It was then that one of the guys pointed out that I should avoid that area 'over there, as it was wet'. Then I realised that I had one soggy sock, oh yes, he said, the carpet was wet by the entrance, I went over to the left and was promptly informed, not to go there because it was leaking. The melting snow on the roof was now dripping onto the carpet.

I eventually found a dry spot, proceeded to unpack and get changed into some dry kit, once that was done I got into the sleeping bag, because I was freezing and needed to warm up. I lay there and thought to myself, that, like so many things in life, first impressions were the wrong impression. I looked at the yurt and thought how comfortable and cosy it was, the reality was that it was a freezing, leaking monstrosity. Ah well, at least I got a dry spot, other runners were now slowly filling the thing, all equally keen to avoid the wet patches.

After a couple of hours, space was becoming a premium and with up to 36 people having to sleep in the thing, it was becoming a little crowded.

I was now nice and warm and, with the sun now coming out to play, I decided to make full use of the sunshine by drying my damp shoes, socks and any other kit that would benefit!

Riz arrived and was unfortunate in that there was only the smallest of spaces left, the space that no one had wanted. It would be fair to say that Riz was a little less than impressed with the overcrowded, damp sleeping conditions – he informed me that he was off to try and find somewhere a little more comfortable. Twenty minutes later, he was back with the news that owing to the overcrowding an extra small yurt had now become available and he was off to sleep in that one. Helping Riz move by carrying some of his stuff over to his new home, I was impressed. Not only was his yurt dry with a raised sleeping platform, it was smaller, had a small log burner and had room for another one or two. I immediately claimed a space and promptly fetched my kit over.

Warm and dry and with a great night's sleep, the morning looked promising with clearish skies, the hustle and bustle of getting ready for the day's run. It was whilst packing away the last few items into my rucksack, that I spotted, falling, oh so gently from the sky, what appeared to be snow flakes. 'Ere we go again!

Stage 2

In the Footsteps of Ghengis Khan

With the thoughts of 'ere we go again, I, along with the others, made my way over to the start line, to get ready for this morning's briefing.

It was another cold morning and again people stood around listening and shivering, whilst at the same time trying to absorb the information about today's stage.

Unfortunately, my mind had wondered, I was trying to decide on the more important things in life like, do I need another wee and why, oh why, did I ditch my waterproof leggings? Just as I reached a decision about not needing to have a wee, I heard something about climbing up to a mountain top temple and that the weather forecast was not promising.

With the briefing over, the countdown began. We all shuffled forward, the excitable chatter died down, 3, 2, 1 and we were off.

I think the feeling was mutual, we were all glad to be moving and thereby warming up. The area we were running through, could, it would be fair to say, not be classed as particularly attractive: grey, damp and cold.

The terrain was tricky and loose underfoot with numerous little streams that we were all trying our best to avoid, lest we get wet feet.

With so many runners all attempting to avoid the streams, all vying for the best, driest route, concentration was required. I knew that somewhere along the line I would get wet feet but I was determined to hold out for as long as possible.

After a while, the route started to ever so slightly climb, eventually people were forced to walk. I employed my usual tactics of holding out for as long as possible, always trying to avoid walking for as long as I could. The slight climb became less slight and more steep and then, suddenly the more steep became more severe. The whole area was covered in snow. We were now climbing. The path was narrow and steep, any deviation from the path took you into deep soft snow, we were, in effect, in a queue. The runners in front had rather selfishly compacted the snow making it slippery, a problem that was compounded by the fact that my superduper desert shoes were exactly that, desert shoes and not designed for climbing snow-covered mountains. They had little or no traction, making every step a little hazardous. The climb seemed never-ending, occasionally someone would stop for a breather, when this happened you needed to be alert, so close were they and so steep was the incline that if someone stopped without warning you, would bump into them. With the owner's bottom inches from your face when you were moving, the sudden stop could have been a little embarrassing to see the least. We clambered up until eventually the incline levelled and stopped and, then and there, we had reached the summit.

With the snow-covered Tian Shan Alpine Temple to our left it was, I'm sure a beautiful temple, a temple that attracts people from miles around. I, unfortunately, couldn't really appreciate the aesthetic beauty of the place. To me, it was nothing more than a marker which had marked the end of the climb.

The descent was gradual and very welcome. The route seemed to be taking us down a small road, wet under foot and a pleasant change from the climbing, every so often we passed a small road crew. There were crews of workmen everywhere, all busy – well, would have been busy, had they not found a certain fascination with the crazy multi-coloured stream of runners passing though, repairing or improving the road. Every so often there was a small campsite, tents in which the workers stayed for the duration of the road works.

I plodded along on legs that were anything but impressed with the downhill section. The only relief they had from the constant downhill pounding was when I had to leap over the numerous small streams that cut across the road.

Groups of workers seemed to be strategically placed to watch the unwary or the unfortunate runner get wet feet, annoying for the runner concerned, but bloody funny for the audience, which I noticed were all, without exception, smoking.

I got overtaken by a couple of runners, then I noticed coming toward me a flock of sheep with a shepherd on horseback – no sheepdog required, just a whip, which he cracked with alarming regularity. It was an impressive display of dog-free sheep-herding, then I saw a sheep riding a motorbike, well a bloke smoking while giving a sheep a lift on a motorbike.

As we dropped down off the mountain, the snow had all but disappeared, the second checkpoint came and went. I left the checkpoint and started walking. I was now in my familiar role of walk a bit, run a bit and the fact that I had somehow managed to keep both feet dry was a bonus. The terrain was a little easier under foot but the poor old legs had taken a battering with a cruel climb and long technical descent the -they had earned the right to have a little rest. I was also very conscious of the fact that this was only day two of this 6 day race.

I knew that these early stages only had three checkpoints – after check point three the next stop was the camp, so I was pleased when checkpoint three came into view. I again made quick use of it and with just 9 km or a little over five miles to the final campsite, I resumed my running.

After about 50 minutes, I spotted a rider on horseback then I saw the world's scruffiest camel, it looked like a half-sheared sheep, great clumps of long, matted hair hanging off it, bald patches and a pissed off look. Fortunately, the pissed-off-looking camel wanted nothing to do with us and trotted off.

I carried on plodding along, spotted what appeared to be a collection of small buildings,I'd remembered that the next campsite was called Shepherds Haven and was in a village. I really hoped that this was it. As I got closer, the place got busier, men on horseback, smoking and rounding up horses and sheep, then climbing the final short incline was the welcome sight of the big red Gobi March finishing banner.

Crossing the finishing line, I felt surprisingly good. I was asked what my tent number was and then was directed to what appeared to be a small garden shed which was in fact a house. Once inside there were a collection of small rooms, each of which was warm, cosy and very inviting. Making my way over to one of the rooms I grabbed one of the more comfortable looking sleeping areas, which, like the yurts were on a raised platform.

The Gobi March Race seemed to have taken over the whole village. Other runners were slowly drifting in to camp. Some looked desperately tired but somehow the actual relief of finishing a stage always makes even the most tired, most knackered and the most grumpy individual smile. It might only be a quick smile but it's a very important smile nonetheless.

Once our little room for the night was filled to its capacity, war stories exchanged, kit sorted, food eaten and the various ailments discussed and treated, it was at last time for lights out.

Stage 3

The Foothills of Tian Shan

After a great night's sleep, it was all too soon that the familiar early morning, choral cacophony of fidgeting and farting woke me up. The good thing about these races is that you never need to set an alarm to wake you, you have absolutely no chance whatsoever of oversleeping. The morning camp ritual of most stage races is usually the same. After waking to the noises of coughing, packing, zipping and unzipping of numerous sleeping bags, some poor sod asking the question "Have you seen my thingy?" and "'I'm sure I had it, last night," "I've got another blister, I wish I had more Sudacrem," etc, etc.

I eventually prised myself away from the warmth of my sleeping bag, grabbed my toothbrush, single-rationed wet wipe and breakfast which consisted of a coffee sachet, a cup and spoon and made my way outside. After washing, face first, always wash face first when only one wet wipe is available (girls might have a different system or several wet wipes) With teeth cleaning and washing out of the way, I made my way over to one of the hot water urns and sat savouring the warm sweet coffee whilst people-watching and looking at today's course notes. Walking back to the room, I realised that since the hotel at Hami, I had not needed to use the race camp toilet. Now, the race camp toilet of any stage race, is a rite of passage, one of life's must do experiences. I armed myself with the necessary, i.e. toilet paper and wet wipes and sauntered off, a man on a mission. I approached the telephone box- shaped canvas cubicle, full of trepidation, much like walking into the dentists, you know it's got to be done, but you also know it's going to be a painful experience.

Once I had reached the two empty cubicles, I knew from bitter experience what to expect. Consequently, I needed to check things out and I opted for the one on the right, only because, it was slightly less full than the one on the left! Decision made, I went in, now the hard work could begin, with quads that felt they had been tenderised, a knee that hurt like hell and a pair of shorts around my ankles that were now acting more like a hobble, thereby seriously limiting any mobility. I adopted the squat position, a position that was uncomfortable. With shaking legs, my aim was compromised, fortunately luck was on my side, it was a bullseye, and with the mission complete, I sauntered off back to the room to finish packing.

Not long after, we were warned that the race briefing would take place in 5 minutes and that we were to start making our way to the start line. I was still in the process of deciding what to wear, would we again encounter snow, it didn't feel as cold as the previous two mornings so I, being an optimist, opted not to put on my rain jacket.

Making my way to the starting area, I thought to myself how lucky I was to be here and as an added bonus, I felt good, no aches, pains or blisters, plus it wasn't raining or snowing, so I had no need to put my coat on, yet!

The countdown began and then we were off, the forward shuffle became a little quicker then, shortly after starting, we reached a dirt road, which allowed us all a bit more room and then we all sort of found our natural place in the race. The front running, racing snakes left us all behind, I sort of settled somewhere in the middle bunch and the slower, more sensible runners settled in behind.

The area we were running through was green, almost grassy-moorland-like and very unlike a desert. Reaching checkpoint one, it was the usual routine of removing the top of my water bottle and topping it up, even though I had only taken a couple of sips, I make it a point of always keeping my water bottle topped up.

As usual, the crew were supportive and helpful, they encouraged each of us. Shortly after leaving the checkpoint, we reached what appeared to be a dried-up river bed. It was tricky and technical, always being a bit of a careless fairy when it comes to running downhill, I had to watch myself and concentrate on each footstep but being chased by runners that were rapidly gaining on me in a very narrow channel, the inevitable happened: I went arse over apex, rolled a couple of times, grazed my hand and knee, instantly got up and pretended to the runners behind who were no doubt desperately trying to stifle their laughs, that everything was fine and that no real damage had been done. Then I thought, bollocks, I hope that I haven't punctured my inflatable mattress. I had done this in a race called the Augrabies Extreme. It was bloody annoying and had left me having a few, very uncomfortable nights.

Once out of the dried-out river bed, the terrain got a little rocky, nothing too difficult but, with my bleeding hand and knee, I had a constant visual reminder to be careful and concentrate. Eventually we reached a fairly decent road that took us past some small villages and then on to the next checkpoint.

Again, it was a quick top-up and leave, the terrain was a little easier and appeared to be an old 4x4 track, it was good to finally be able to settle down with a consistent steady pace. After about 4 or 5 miles the route took us onto a proper road. I normally hate road running but once on the glorious asphalt, I felt duty-bound to try speed up and take advantage of the asphalt.

As per usual, the speeding up part was just wishful thinking. However, I did manage to catch a couple of runners, not because of my incredible burst of speed, but purely because I was able to hang onto my plod longer than they could hang on to theirs.

Approaching another village, I hoped that the checkpoint was close, checkpoint number three was the last checkpoint before camp. Some of the locals lined the road, watching us, the men smoking, the women with bemusement and the kids seemingly confused.

Once through the village, we were guided onto another 4x4 track and told that the checkpoint was about 1 km away which was good news because it had started to rain. It wasn't particularly heavy rain and it wasn't particularly windy but the breeze, rain combination had a nasty chilling effect that had made me start to feel cold. I finally caught the runner that I had been following for some time – it turned out to be my fellow tent companion Richard.

We plodded along, chatting away, and then spotted the checkpoint, and not before time. The heavens had opened and I was now freezing. Once we reached the checkpoint, I removed my rucksack and started faffing about, Richard, being more organised, left just before me. I needed to not only put my raincoat on, but my gloves as well. I was shivering and knew I wouldn't be able to run fast enough to get warm and my rather economical plodding pace would only manage to prevent me getting any colder than I already was.

The short stop had left me freezing, but with only about 8 miles to the camp site, I decided to run, well plod without stopping, if only to get warmer.

This particular part of the route continued along the same 4x4 track. Though the going was relatively easy, the fact that it was raining hard had meant that the dark, rain-lashed landscape now appeared to be bloody ugly or maybe it was just me, fed up with the rain and moaning to myself about being bloody wet in a bloody desert, a bloody pain. I carried on with my slow auto plod, passed a couple of other runners who looked as fed up with the rain as I was.

I caught up with Richard, had a quick chat and slowly inched ahead, desperate to finish.

Though we were still on a well-defined track that seemed to go on for miles, I was very conscious of the fact that it was the pink marker flags that we should be following and not the well-defined track – it would be all to easy to switch off and just follow the track, I had made that mistake once before and wasn't about to repeat it, so I kept a very careful eye on the little pink flags. It was just as well because they disappeared to the right and away from the track.

The guy ahead kept disappearing from view, a bit like a ball floating in a rough sea, one minute you could see it, then it disappeared into the next wave's trough.

Small, annoying undulations made forward progress exactly that annoyingly slow. My progress was now slow enough to make me feel the cold, I desperately scanned the horizon ahead, looking for any clue as to the whereabouts of the campsite, but nothing. All I saw was the little pink marker flags and a disappearing runner who seemed to be pulling away from me.

I decided to treat myself to a high energy sports jelly bean then I heard what I thought was thunder. The continuous thundering didn't stop and sounded more like an amateurish drum solo, only then did the penny drop that it was the finish line.

This race was slightly unusual because it was the one race I had done that you actually heard the finish line before you saw it. One of the race crew had, for whatever reason, bought a rather large bongo drum that was now beaten with enthusiastic fury by a member of the support crew every time someone approached and crossed the finish line. Possibly annoying for the first finishers of the day who had to listen to a furiously enthusiastic cacophony up to a 160 times, but for the runner crossing the finish line, the bongo-playing made even the most knackered, most fed up and most in pain runner smile.

I crossed the finish, wearing that same smile and was disappointed to see that the tents were back, having been rather spoilt with the yurts and then the village house it was now sadly back to basics.

I found our tent, which was empty, which in turn meant that I was the first one in. I took the opportunity to strip off my wet kit, no easy task when shaking and shivering. Just as I was about to remove the last of my wet garments, in walked Richard, who was now confronted with a semi-naked, shivering Englishman standing in the middle of the tent. We were both far too polite to think that the situation was anything but normal, but I was also very aware of the cold weather doing me absolutely no favours, if you know what I mean.

Once I got into some dry kit, I made myself a hot drink and then made my way over to one of the small campfires. It was interesting sitting by the fire, changing roles from runner to spectator, watching a steady procession of slightly soggy, very bedraggled, garish-clad runners. Runners that now had the appearance of homeless vagrants, wearing anything that might just keep the elements at bay – cheap plastic ponchos, torn, tied and tucked in, in a desperate rather forlorn attempt to keep the rain out. A couple had even used their emergency foil survival blanket, some limped across the finish line, some walked, some ran, but every one of them, no matter what they were wearing, wore a huge smile.

As the runners came in, so the rain eased off and with it the chance, all be it a small chance, of drying some kit, tents were quickly converted into improvised clothes lines. Socks, pants, shorts, bras, gloves and coats were all hung out to dry on any available space. It wasn't long before the whole campsite took on the image of refugee camp,

Limping bodies, covered in an assortment of dressings, milling around, trying to find a friend or something to eat and drink. As the last of the runners made their way into camp, and with the light fading, I made myself a meal and another hot drink, pleased with the fact that I had managed to dry most of my kit, was racing well and had no immediate problem. I felt good, no stiffness, soreness or blisters, so far so good.

Stage 4

Crossing the Hami Express

After another good night's sleep, it was up to the usual dawn chorus and getting dressed, I realised that my running top wasn't as dry as I had thought. I now had the horrible sensation of putting a cold damp shirt on. I grabbed my usual morning coffee, sat for a few moments savouring the hot drink, whilst watching the campsite and checking my feet.

It's funny how. on any desert stage races, we all become slightly fixated on our feet, a desert stage race is really just a crash course in chiropody. We can patch up, diagnose, drain and dress blisters, remove toe nails and clean wounds.

We were literally in the shadow of the Tian Shan Mountains and looking down to where the route would be taking us, it looked very flat – miles and miles of very flat. However, the sun, something that had thus far been hiding from us, was, for now, shining on the route that we would shortly be running. I really hoped that the terrain was as flat as it looked and that the sun was here to stay.

I returned to the tent and packed up. It was now day four and my rucksack still felt as heavy as it did on day one. Once the packing and moaning to myself were done, I made my way over to the start line and briefing. This time, however, we were sort of nearly reassured that the weather would be better as would the terrain and with the distance being just 42 km, (26.3 miles) it was slightly shorter than yesterday. Today, I decided, was going to be a good day.

As the countdown began and the last few stragglers appeared from tents and toilets, 3, 2, 1, and we were off. Keeping the mountains to our right, we plodded along on a sort of gravel track that was just very slightly climbing. Then we started to descend ever so slowly and then, almost without realising it, we were running through wide open, stony desert terrain. Once away from the mountains it seemed to get warmer, I was moving well and possibly a little too fast – just too fast for me to maintain the pace for long and I was now getting hot and decided on a quick drink. Bollocks, it was only now that I realised that I had left my water bottle behind. Do I go back? Or do I go on? Decisions, decisions, how the hell had I forgotten my water bottle? It wasn't as though it was tucked away inside my rucksack: it was actually a handheld water bottle, designed to be carried in my hand.

I did the maths, we were possibly 3/4 km from the start line, to go back would make it 6/8 km and then to return to where I am now would make it an extra 9/12km, several extra miles that I really didn't need. Sod that, I'll go thirsty, at least I had my Camelbak which contained my electrolyte drink. I plodded along, happy with my decision, but annoyed with my stupidity.

The first checkpoint thankfully came into view, the ever-supportive crew were ready and instantly handed me a bottle of water which I gratefully took with me, realising that each checkpoint was roughly between 6 and 7 miles. I figured that water bottles handed out at each checkpoint were just about enough to get me through to each of them, well, that's the theory. Once I left the checkpoint, I quickly got into my usual, comfortable, plodding pace. The terrain was flat and rocky with the occasional small bush, unfortunately, the easy flat stuff, like so many things in life comes at a price and the price was relentless, boring, hours of monotony.

I was almost glad when someone passed me, it gave me a few

moments of distraction.

A team from China were fascinating in that respect, resplendent in their red and white team colours, they looked professional and slick, running past at a great rate of knots and in a single file, metronomic unison, their impressive speed and team work was a joy to watch. However the confusing thing about this team was the fact they would go flying past like a steam train, only for me to catch them up as they stopped to take pictures, crack jokes, have a break and generally piss about. I would slowly pass them and then half an hour later or so. they would resume their professional demeanour and go storming past in perfect unison. I was enviously watching them go storming past for the umpteenth time when I was suddenly aware that up ahead were a couple of Police vehicles. The Police presence continued to be an ever-watching eye and just seemed to appear out of nowhere. Now, however, they were either guarding a road or guiding us across the road, which saw us tackling a small nasty little climb – once across the road it was back, onto the flat and finally, the next checkpoint.

Again the crew saw us through quickly and without fuss. Not long after leaving checkpoint number three, we headed to an underpass which took us under a main road and once again, the ever present Police were watching and guiding us.

It was now getting bloody hot, I was slowing down and drinking too much but I wasn't overly worried because with less than 7 miles until the finish line, I knew I would get there in less than a couple of hours. Following the marker flags, I was suddenly overtaken by a couple of runners, who then disappeared under an underpass that went under the Hami Express railway line and again there was another Police presence. They were either watching us with a great degree of interest or slightly baffled, bemusement.

I saw the two runners that had overtaken me disappear under the railway line and, keen to put on a good show of impressive Ultra distance running for the Police, went to follow them. Unfortunately, I again made a complete tit of myself, by trying to get under the low, the very low underpass, my 6 foot four inch height with rucksack was preventing me from crouching low enough in a five foot high underpass and I had to make a tactical withdrawal, back out and remove my rucksack then, like the hunchback of bleeding Notre Dame, sort of sidle my way through, carrying my rucksack in my hand – dignified, it was not.

As I sneaked a backward glance, I noticed a couple of the Police officers were peering through the underpass, no doubt amused at the comedy unfolding before them, so funny did they find the spectacle that I'm sure I heard the muffled sound of stifled laughter.

Once through to the other side, it was back on to the flat, rocky stuff. On the distant horizon, I could see trees and greenery, eventually the small rocks were replaced by sand-like silt. It looked as though a fast-flowing torrent had passed through, fortunately, the heat of the sun had baked it just hard enough for it to become a half-decent running surface.

As the greenery and the trees got closer, I focused like a sniper, intently scanning horizon, desperately looking for any clue that would confirm the presence of the campsite: nothing. However, on closer inspection, I did spot movement, people busy going about their business.

Just before the tree line was a small, sloped stone wall that looked as though it had been constructed to channel a fast-flowing river. Once on top, it was a case of following a small track through what was obviously now cultivated, agricultural land, irrigation ditches and pipes were all around. The route markers took us on to the top of a man-made bank, before we dropped back down and through another small underpass, again, guarded by the ubiquitous, smoking Police officers.

Once through to the other side, the track led us through a maze of vineyards, a few workers were working and smoking away and then, as I turned a corner I spotted a runner up ahead, following the route through the maze of vineyards and irrigation ditches. I saw a labourer who was busy opening the sluice gates that allowed the water to be free and thus flood the immediate area, with a few inches of water the runner ahead wasn't quick enough and the now wet, sandy, silty gloop-like mud trapped the poor, unfortunate runner. Luckily for me, I spotted an escape route and, as the unfortunate runner made his way back to me wearing what appeared to be heavy lead diving boots, I took full advantage of the runner's sad demise and nipped up onto a smaller slightly-raised concrete shallow irrigation channel – it was dry and unused but made the perfect footpath.

Just as I had taken advantage of the runner in front, so the two runners behind took advantage of my sneaky navigational route-finding and promptly followed me.

Once off the small section of irrigation channel, it was down to flatter, less cultivated terrain and then onto a small road. It was then that I spotted a couple of the support crew enthusiastically cheering us on. It was good to see them as it meant the finish line was close. Determined to look the part of impressive Ultra distance running machine, I speeded up and sprinted for the finish line. Unfortunately, however, the support crew brought me down to earth with a rather large bump, as they said well done, looking good, looking strong and the finish line is only a couple of km away. Bravado and ego prevented me from slowing down too soon, but when I heard the crew clapping and cheering the two runners behind me, I knew it was safe to slow down without looking a complete prat.

I carried on, albeit at a more sedate, sensible pace and then, just as Jim Reeves himself would say I heard the sound of distant drums. Picking out, up ahead, a small collection of what appeared to be ruined buildings, with the slightly bonkers bongo bashing, increasing in intensity the nearer I got, before finally hitting a crescendo as I, at last, crossed the finish line.

This campsite was called Spring Village, a misnomer if ever there was one. There was nothing either spring-like or village-like about the small collection of sun-baked, ruined, mud- built buildings that made up our little campsite, the village. It would be fair to say that it had a certain rustic charm and it was that charm that made the collection of ruined buildings somehow cosy and, as an added bonus, the ruins afforded us a little shaded protection from the intensity of the day's heat, not that we were housed in the buildings but the tents we were in were often in the shadow of those buildings. Runners and support crew were in one area and the huge contingent of Police and military personnel were in the other. As runners continued to come in, the drumming continued, the camp slowly filled with relieved-looking runners, the medics tent had a constant and regular supply of fresh blisters to treat.

Stage 5

The Long March

The Long March, was someone's attempt at humour. A homage perhaps to Mao Zedong's infamous Long March, a march of ten thousand Li (5000 km approx), so brutal that many never made it. Were we about to suffer a similar, but hopefully slightly less brutal, Long March?

152 of us remained, 152 of us made our way over to the start line, ready for the morning briefing. A fantastic kaleidoscope of colourful runners was now on show, runners covered in an assortment of colourful KT Tape®, bright tops, garish shorts, leggings, hats, packs and shades were on full display. A complete mixture of emotion was also on show, for many 80km or roughly 50 miles was the longest single run they had ever done and this would have to be done carrying a pack and on top of the four previous tough days, four days of being battered by snowstorms and rainstorms. Some were subdued into silence, others were nervous and chatty and some, like me, were lost in a private world of thought, unfortunately, my own private thoughts were anything but philosophical and are usually littered with expletives, along the line of oh shit!

The race briefing confirmed what we had already suspected, it was going to be bloody hot, at last proper desert heat. Large amounts of sun cream were frantically applied, water bottles were filled, final checks made. As the countdown began, final words of wisdom from the race crew were passed on, things like, don't forget to drink plenty and keep any bare skin covered up!

I made final adjustments to my pack, made sure my Camelbak was working, my nibbles were ready and to hand, shoes not too tight, sun glasses and hat were just right, 3,2,1 and we were once again off.

For most of us, the start was a slow, apprehensive shuffle, the previous tough four days of running were now on show, strange gaits betrayed those trying to hide blisters, chaffing, sore muscles and God knows what else, but we all crept forward, except, that was, for the racing snakes, who shot off, keen to get on with the very serious business of racing whilst the rest of us were getting on with the equally serious business of surviving.

It was good to get moving but I was very aware of the distance ahead and consequently, forced myself to tuck in behind anyone I thought was being sensible. I planned to reach the first couple of checkpoints relatively comfortably then slowly start increasing the pace, well, that was my rather optimistic theory.

Fortunately, the terrain was runner-friendly: though slightly sandy, it was not in the least bit hilly, or, as any race organiser calls it, undulating. The further away from the mountains we got the more the Gobi changed into what it should have been all along, a desert, a proper desert, with sand, blue skies and heat.

I was just appreciating the fact that I was now getting into the proper desert, when up ahead and somewhat out of place, were the huge concrete columns that supported the elevated railway line that the Hami Express bullet train was now thundering along, the passengers from their elevated, privileged position must have wondered what on earth was happening far below in the desert, a swarm of colourful runners, like ants scurrying along the desert floor before disappearing under the train they were riding along in.

Not long after passing under the railway, we approached a small village and again people cheered and clapped as we approached the first of the seven checkpoints that we needed to reach.

I was still running (sort of) and was keen to maintain a run, albeit a slow run for as long as possible. I was very aware of the distance and the fact that the heat would intensify making the chance of me doing anything but plod along, for most of this stage, highly unlikely.

It wasn't long after leaving the checkpoint that we dropped down off our slightly elevated position onto or, rather, into what the race organisers had called the Vast Black Gobi Desert Landscape. It certainly looked vast. Vast, flat and rocky.

Picking out the line of small pink marker flags, it was head down, arse in gear time, mental preparation for the many miles of monotony that lay ahead. One flag at a time, one check point down six to go. On long stages or races, I always try and break the whole thing down into bite size manageable chunks, to look too far ahead and actually think about how much further there is to go, would make the whole thing rather unpleasant and seemingly impossible. I might just about make the next checkpoint but I would never make the finish line. So every time I leave a checkpoint, I put all my effort into reaching the next and then the next and so on, until finally the next one becomes the last one.

Plodding along trying to reach the next flag, I spotted a runner ahead, which was great because it now gave me something else to focus on other than the bloody pink flags. Watching the runner ahead, I adopted my usual cunning masterplan and decided to just follow and not overtake, no matter how fast they were moving I would remain behind, this, I hoped, would keep me in check, preventing me from either going too fast or too slow.

Unfortunately for me, the runner in front must have realised that the bloke behind was using his pace to carry him along. His pace was inconsistent, sometimes he seemed to be setting a pace that I was struggling to keep up with and then suddenly he would be moving so slowly that I had to check myself so as not to get too close. This cat and mouse game carried on, occasionally the runner would stop and hunch over with hands on knees, he appeared to be struggling and then just as I got close enough to him he would stand up straight and shoot off.

This rather strange charade carried on until I reached the next checkpoint, it was only then that I realised that the guy really was struggling as the support crew set to work on him, removing his backpack, spraying him with cool water and rehydrating him with electrolytes. He seemed to be in a desperate state. Me, being the mercenary bastard that I am, of course took full advantage of his distressed state and left the checkpoint immediately.

Plodding along, eating a couple of jelly babies in celebration of my rather dubious tactics, smug in the knowledge that I had gained one place, I now decided that I would get to the next checkpoint, which was a little under six miles away without being caught by any runner. I tried to speed up but, as usual, failed miserably.

Suddenly, and out of nowhere, came the runner that I had last seen looking somewhat the worse for wear at the checkpoint, he had made an amazing recovery and had obviously decided that I was a cheeky bastard who needed to be taught a lesson, Fair point, I let him carry on, the fact that there was no way on earth I could have done anything about it anyway helped. As I was busy admiring the runner's impressive turn of speed, just to add insult to injury, one of the Chinese runners came storming past.

So much for my trying to get to checkpoint three without being overtaken, the unfortunate thing was that there was really nothing I could do about it anyway. I was now into what I call auto plod, a pace that I had no choice but to maintain. I could not, no matter hard I tried, speed up, the only positive thing was that it was a comfortable pace that I knew I could maintain.

As I finally reached checkpoint three, I was momentarily confused. It was one of those 'deja vu' moments, the runner that had made such a miraculous recovery earlier on and had come storming past me was once again having major work done on him with the crew spraying him with cool water and rehydrating him as he sat in the shade of the gazebo. It looked more like a Formula 1 pit stop with the driver's team frantically working on him, I did what I had done before, grabbed my water and left.

Checkpoint four beckoned, so I left immediately. The heat was intense and it seemed to be getting hotter, it's always tricky when racing through deserts, should I go fast and get the thing over with as quickly as possible but run the risk of overheating, or do I go slower so as not to over heat but spend more time in the heat?

I was busy working all this out, when I was suddenly aware of a runner coming up behind me, Richard my Kiwi tent-mate had caught me. He seemed strong, looked good and was chatty. We chatted for a few minutes, but in that few minutes I realised that he was keen to press ahead and take advantage of the feeling good moment, (those moments normally don't last long, so always take advantage when you have one). I didn't mind, as he pulled away from me I tried to speed up, tried to keep him in sight but couldn't. I let him go, safe in the knowledge that I would catch him later as I had done almost everyday thus far.

The area of the Gobi we were now in was stunning, wide, open and vast, huge rock formations carved into weird and wonderful shapes, by nothing more than many thousands of years of wind and sand, sand-blasted and beautiful.

Reaching checkpoint four, I fully expected to see Richard sitting there, unfortunately, he had gone. I still felt reasonably good, nothing hurt and though it was hot it was nothing that I had not experienced many times before, nothing I could not manage so I figured that I could catch Richard. I left the checkpoint with one aim in mind, to catch Richard.

It was head down, grind out time. Following the little pink marker flags and taking small regular sips of water with the occasional electrolyte drink, I maintained what I thought was a reasonable pace until, that was, two runners came storming past, Chris and Sam, more tent-mates. They both looked really strong, whereas I felt knackered and had no energy. Being passed didn't bother me, I was used to that but being passed so easily and the fact that I was unable to speed up or react even just a little bit must have knocked my confidence. This lack of energy, unable to speed up had only happened once before during a race and that was in the 430 mile Yukon Arctic Ultra. I watched enviously as the pair of them disappeared into the distance, I now just focused on reaching checkpoint five, which I really hoped I could do without being passed by anyone else.

I plodded along, occasionally looking up and around and thought to myself this place should be bloody ugly with so little here, just stones, rocks and sky and yet it was beautiful. The rolling, stony terrain, occasionally broken up by strangely-fascinating sculptured monolithic rock formations, framed by a beautiful blue sky. I was lucky to be here and felt even luckier when I spotted, just up ahead, checkpoint number five.

On reaching the checkpoint, I grabbed a chair. I was knackered and in desperate need of a seat. Samantha asked if I was ok in the heat, knowing I much prefer racing in the Arctic. I confirmed what she already knew, I prefer minus 45 as opposed to the plus 45. After 10/15 minutes or so, I hauled my carcass off the chair and left the checkpoint, five down two to go.

Following the track and the flags I pushed on and, within an hour, I realised that I was bollocksed and struggling to maintain any forward momentum. I was weakening by the minute. Nothing hurt, no blisters, no chaffing, I had been drinking and eating enough but, out of nowhere, my already limited energy reserves were being depleted, my already very slow pace was now getting slower. I had somehow, and without realising it, stepped into a world of misery.

I have had moments like this before during races but they were exactly that: moments. This misery moment felt as if it were here to stay. In fact, negative thoughts started to make their presence felt, negative thoughts are undoubtedly the Ultra runner's worst enemy, far worse than blisters or nausea, fear or monotony, these usually pass, get treated or managed, negative thoughts are destructive, eroding and powerful. It can start by asking the simple question why, why am I doing this, it's a bloody waste of time, I don't have anything to prove, I could have spent my hard-earned money on something else. In fact it is a waste of time and a waste of money and besides, my feet hurt. If I carry on, I could be crippled for life, it's too far, it's too hot, it's dangerous to continue, in fact when I see someone from the support crew

I'll tell them that I've finished because I don't really want to be crippled for life and I'll explain that I won't, can't possibly continue with all the problems I have. Then, just as you have reached that monumental decision, a 4X4 race support vehicle approaches, you smile, wave enthusiastically, they pull up and say you're looking good, doing really well. It's not far until the next checkpoint, then for some bizarre reason you say thanks and they drive off and you carry on, having both lied to each other. I carried on and, whilst walking along, my head dropped for the umpteenth time, which was, I decided either a sign of fatigue, depression or quite possibly both. So, whilst unable to look at anything but my shoes a thought occurred, bollocks, I've ruined another pair of perfectly good training shoes, I'll have to throw them away when I get back to the hotel. With thoughts about the price of buying a new pair of training shoes, I took another swig of the warm water and realised that I had been drinking far faster than I had thought, my bottle was nearly empty – now to add to my list of woes, the possibility of dehydration. I scoured the route ahead for any signs of the checkpoint, more in hope than anything else, nothing.

Following the pink flags was the only thing that kept me going. One flag at a time was all I could manage, then as I approached a small but steep hill, I spotted on the top what I hoped was the checkpoint and not before time. With the greatest of effort I hauled myself up to the top only to realise that it wasn't a checkpoint but just a single 4x4 support vehicle, my disappointment was short-lived when the driver offered me a bottle of much-needed water. I was desperate and grateful for the chance to stop, if only briefly. It had to be brief because thoughts of The Clashes 1982 hit Should I stay or Should I go?' started to raise some very serious questions like should I stay or should I go?

As I was taking another swig of water, a couple of runners crested the hill, one was blind and the other was his guide. So impressive, I suddenly felt very ashamed of myself, there was I moping about feeling sorry for myself, then this blind runner turns up looking fresh and was actually enjoying himself and couldn't have been happier. They left within seconds, I left shortly after, feeling ever so slightly ashamed. Watching them disappear ahead, I wondered if

I would have had the balls to try a race like this if I lost my sight and decided that I probably wouldn't.

As I approached yet another, small challenging hill, I looked at it and wondered if I would actually manage to reach the top. At about halfway up I found the answer, no, not without a rest, I stopped hunched over and, with my hands on my knees, tried to compose myself. I felt absolute exhaustion. Just as I was in the process of moving off, a support vehicle appeared and a photographer got out, took a couple of photos and then informed me that the checkpoint was just around the corner. I moved off and was so relieved when I saw checkpoint 6, grabbing a quick seat I figured that with just 10 km to go before reaching the last checkpoint, I would move as soon as I could which was fortunately after about 10 minutes.

The heat seemed to be doing a lot of damage and had certainly made me suffer, I just hoped that I could reach the next checkpoint. Having to rely on hope rather than ability was a sure sign that things were not going well. All I could do now was put one foot in front of the other for the next 10 kms and when I finally approached Checkpoint 7, I realised that I really, really needed checkpoint seven, I was chin-strapped, bollocksed, hanging on and desperate. I needed a couple of minutes to compose myself. I grabbed a seat and did something I have very rarely done and certainly never done at the last checkpoint of any race: I faffed about in my rucksack, in desperate need of my last 'for goodness shakes' recovery drink. I sat down, savouring the delicious strawberry-flavoured life saving drink, whilst contemplating such things as why am I here, not the core philosophical question of why are we born, but why am I here faffing about in the desert, what am I doing and will I manage to finish? Each of those questions were answered as quickly as they were asked, I'm here because I was lucky to be, because I wanted to be. What am I doing ? What else would I be doing and I'm doing what I wanted to do and finally, bloody right, I'll finish.

As I sat there, a couple of runners came and went. Disappointed that I was once again being overtaken and even more disappointed that there was sod all I could about it. I had to use every ounce of willpower I possessed to haul my knackered old carcass off the chair, I must have looked more pitiful than I thought because one of the support crew helped me on with my rucksack and, as a final humiliation, she commented on how light my pack was compared to some of the others. She was either a powerlifter with an extraordinary ability to lift heavy weights or I had now turned into a feeble wretch, suffering from a debilitating form of lethargy.

I left the checkpoint, knowing that I had just 10km to go. Not long after leaving the relative comfort of the checkpoint, I had to switch on my head-torch. The terrain was nice and flat, the easiest that we had had all day. Occasionally, I would look up, desperate for any sign of the finish line, tiredness or desperation were playing tricks on me with the occasional snatched glimpse of moving lights. Being an old hand at this racing malarkey, I wasn't falling for it, I knew better than to think for one moment that the finish line was actually within sight.

At between 22:00 and 22:30 I definitely saw lights, real unmistakable lights, they seemed to me to be the headlights on a moving vehicle. Satisfied that they were real and not a figment of my befuddled imagination, I started to think that I might just might be able to reach the end.

As I inched my way forward, the lights became more prevalent and then the unmistakable sound of beautiful bongo bashing at its cacophonous best. The flat terrain suddenly ended and a slight but challenging incline had to be negotiated. It seemed to go on for a while, but the lights and bongo bashing drew me on until I spotted the finishing banner, wonderfully illuminated from behind. As I got closer, the drums got louder, reaching fever pitch as I finally crossed the line, claps and cheers all round, water given and directions to my tent. Thankfully, being tent number one meant that it was the nearest.

I was the fourth one into our tent, the others looked annoyingly fresh, but we were all wearing huge smiles.

During the rest of the night the bongo-bashing continued,

reaching a crescendo every time a runner crossed the line.

Camp life. Statues of the Black Gobi

As the sun rose high above the campsite and the stragglers continued to finish, the campsite's beauty was revealed, stunning and surrounded by huge carved rock formations, streaked and pitted after many a millennia of sand-blasting. Now that same wind that was responsible for carving and shaping those mighty monoliths was doing its utmost to flatten our campsite. Tents that now behaved more like sails, were flapping violently, with runners and race support crew fighting a losing battle to keep them from being blown over. One by one, the wind claimed victory, eventually every one of the tents was left lying like a pile of discarded rags, rags that were slowly but surely being buried by the windblown sand. The sandy, gritty combination that had so effectively sculpted and carved rock was now sand-blasting each of us. After several hours of relentless battering, and with no protection and no end in sight, we were left with little choice but to withdraw, the only protection available was in the lee of the giant rock formations.

As we all sat huddled in our little groups, we were informed that the maelstrom was not only set to continue for some hours but there was now a sandstorm on its way.

As we settled down to ride out the storm, I noticed that the race photographers and TV crew were getting themselves busy, setting up cameras and picking vantage points to best capture the approaching sandstorm. Natural curiosity got the better of some us and, as we peered around the corner, we could see what all the fuss was about: a huge wall of sand at least a kilometre in height was heading our way, it was huge and moving fast, like watching film footage of the 2004 Tsunami but instead of a wall of water we were looking at a wall of sand.

When it finally hit us, it was a case of hold on tight, cover your mouth and nose. The noise as the sand hit was immense, any exposed skin was now subjected to an extreme form of exfoliation, the type of exfoliation that would not have been out of place in one of those rather strange Japanese game shows.

Once the worst of the storm had passed, we were left with a scene of absolute devastation – the campsite had been flattened, remnants of tents, bits of kit and gazebos lay strewn around a wide area, only prevented from being blown away by the weight of the sand that now half-buried everything. Race crew and runners, Police and security slowly emerged from their respective hidey-holes.

Faces slowly emerged, wide-eyed from behind an assortment of improvised protective visors, sweat-stained, sand-encrusted hair and facial features, bleary eyed survivors taking a few moments to recognise the person before them.

It was now getting dark and people started wandering around the campsite, checking on kit and packs that we had each hidden under the flattened tents. It was, we were informed still too windy to put the tents up and we should really start thinking about sorting our stuff out ready for a night under the stars. No hardship, as I considered that sleeping out in the desert and under the stars was definitely one of life's must-do experiences.

We all made our way to our respective tents, ground sheets only, were made ready for a night under the stars, I lay on my back, hands clasped behind my head, all smug and self-satisfied, looking up and, as beautiful as the night sky was, it was sadly cut short by the ominous rolling cloud that began to look a little menacing, the menace was then confirmed by the pitter-patter of tiny rain drops.

I did what I normally do at a time like this, pretended it wasn't really raining, savoured the comfort of my nice warm sleeping bag and tried to go to sleep, until that was the more sensible amongst us started to get survival bags out and proceeded to protect their sleeping bags from the wet. I followed suit.

Once we were all sorted out, comfortable and cosy, the race staff and crew came around and roused each of us, informing us that preparation was now under way to evacuate the campsite as it now looked as if the weather would get worse and, not only would we be abandoning the camp site, but tomorrows final stage was CANCELLED!

As we started making preparations to leave the camp, I was trying to decide if I was happy about not having to run the 11.8 km or glad that the race was finally over. I remembered the great atmosphere when I finished the Atacama Crossing. The party atmosphere, cheering, clapping, music and pizza but then I thought about yesterdays trial, the hanging on by the skin of my teeth, the effort and willpower to reach the finish line.

The small convoy of vehicles finally arrived and took us to our coaches and then on to the Hami Hotel.

It was a disappointing end to what had been an amazing experience, The Gobi Desert was certainly interestingly extreme, we had been through snowstorms, rainstorms, sandstorms and the baking desert heat. The Gobi March was not by any means the toughest Desert Race out there, but it was certainly one of the more challenging, the adverse weather conditions had made the whole thing a rather unique experience.

What next?

Boys will be boys

How much further?

The sand storm cometh

The Runner's Nuts

Chapter 6
My First Marathon
The London Marathon 1997

What is it?
Possibly the greatest of all the big city marathons

When?
April

Where?
London

Distance:
26.2 miles

It is:
An experience every runner should experience at least once.

See:
www.virginlondonmarathon.com

After eight attempts, I finally managed to get a place in the London Marathon.

Last year, 1996, I had managed to somehow haul my carcass over the finish-line in what was billed as the 'Worlds Toughest Footrace', the Marathon Des Sables. Consequently, I was confident about my ability in finishing a mere marathon.

Arriving in London on the Friday, my ever-loyal wife and I made our way to the London Marathon Exhibition which was at Earls Court. It was packed and extremely well-organised. It took me less than 15 minutes to get registered and more importantly collect my goody bag. Once registered, we could have a good look around the Marathon Exhibition and I managed to spend too much money on stuff that I really needed, well, stuff I thought I really needed, anyway that's what I told my wife. People were handing out flyers about up-and-coming races, little free samples of snacks, lubes, creams, lotions and potions and me never being one to refuse a freebie, took anything and everything that was handed to me. After what was supposed to have been a fairly relaxing day, we returned to the hotel, knackered.

A night of restless sleep, countless trips to the toilet and, before I was really ready, race day had arrived. I tried to eat breakfast but failed. A couple of black coffees and a glass or two of fresh orange juice was all I could manage and then, all too soon, it was time to board the coach that would take us to the start at Blackheath, with the composer Ron Goodwin's the Trap, a piece of music that had now become synonymous with the London Marathon – a theme tune that was instantly recognisable to the thousands of armchair marathon runners – blaring out through the numerous loud speakers. The atmosphere was fantastic, consequently you instantly felt part of something special. More carnival, than race start. Large multi-shaped and multi-coloured advertising balloons, swaying gently above us, tents and toilets everywhere. The tents were providing tea and coffee. Industrial sized urinals and mile-long queues for the portaloos for those more nervous runners, were scattered all around – as the start time for the race got nearer so the toilet queues got longer.

Eventually it was time, time to make my way over to the pen that had been assigned to me. Each runner was allocated a pen that was specific to the runner's estimated time. My estimated time was between 3:30 and 3:45 hours and, looking around at some of the rather rotund individuals, I was beginning to think that some people had got their rather lofty ambitions mixed up with their equally limited capabilities

As I climbed over the railings and squeezed my way through

a mass of nervous bodies, I noticed that there was a very distinctive odour; sweaty nervous bodies, mixed with Deep Heat and flatulence. So tight were we packed that you couldn't help but touch each other, cosy and intimate but at least the closeness of so many bodies meant that it was a little warmer. The tannoy system blared out final instructions to those unfortunates who were still attached to a toilet.

The countdown began for the elite runners at the front. This was our cue to get ready and time to now discard the black bin bag that I was wearing in a forlorn attempt to keep warm.

And, at six foot four inches tall it was somewhat problematic and a little undignified to suddenly have to wrestle my way out of a large black bin bag. A grown man fighting his way out of a bin bag was, I decided, not a good look.

Once the bin bag had been discarded, ie. thrown in the direction of some poor unfortunate spectator, we could begin to shuffle our way forward, small dainty steps like a Japanese geisha. We inch by slow inch crept forward. Finally, after 11 minutes, we reached the start line. I now realised that I was 11 minutes behind my estimated time before I had even started. I made a rather feeble attempt to make up for the lost 11 minutes, however, the stop, start, nature of the first congested mile or so achieved not a lot; in fact, I probably lost even more time.

After three miles or so, the runners that had started in differently-coloured starting areas all merged into one. Consequently, the tightly-packed grouping became less so, gaps appeared and so did the chance to speed up. Every time a small gap presented itself, I sprinted forward and through it, sprint a bit, plod a bit. After a while, space became plentiful and now was the chance to make up the lost time. I went for it, running quickly and confidently, determined to claw back the lost time.

I slowly realised that trying to claw back time was a pretty pointless exercise and I was getting stressed out, trying to achieve the unachievable. I slowed down to what I considered to be a far more sensible/sustainable pace.

The trouble with such an iconic marathon was the fact that we were treated to some amazing and historic sights and, because I had finally managed to get here, I was now determined to enjoy it, savour it, acknowledge the crowds and take in those sights.

So busy was I sightseeing that, when after about six miles the famous Cutty Sark came into view, I was so busy looking at the famous tea clipper and thinking that, while we were in London, we must pay a visit, I failed to notice that a slight incline had suddenly appeared. being naturally lazy, I hadn't picked my feet up and very nearly went arse over apex.

The water stations were plentiful as were the energy drink stations. Each of the stations were fraught with problems. Bunching, people would, and without warning, stop to have a drink and then, just as suddenly, start running again, causing a stop-start bottleneck. Then the discarded bottles would be waiting for the unwary runner to trip over.

After about 12 miles I slowed down, it wasn't my choice to slow down it just sort of happened when I wasn't really looking.

Runners in fancy dress were plodding along more quickly than me and I can assure you that there is nothing more disheartening than a man dressed as a toilet overtaking you, closely followed by a fairy waving a wand and wearing a beard.

The water stations were regular, as were the energy drink stations, the good thing about the energy drink stations was that you could hear them before you reached them. On approaching the stations, there was the sound of a thousand velcro-ripping cheerleaders. The sound wasn't actual cheerleaders (though that would have been very nice), it was the sound of the sticky, sweet energy drink that had been spilled, splashed and discarded along the road – thousands of feet now trudged through a sticky, syrupy-covered road.

The atmosphere was electric, people looking out of windows and cheering, row upon row of spectators lined the street, bands played various kinds of music; jazz, calypso, reggae, pop and rock – every taste catered for.

It was, I decided, one big marathon party, a party that was measured in miles not time, like running through one huge street party. Little kids lined the route, with parents clapping and shouting words of encouragement, the runners high-fiving the outstretched hands, whilst trying not to trip over.

Every so often, one of the spectators would hold out a container with slices of orange, or jelly babies. Occasionally, a small child would offer a piece of chocolate that they had held onto for just a bit too long, in the hope that one of the London Marathon runners would take it. The over-excited child would, no doubt, have held the piece of chocolate too tightly in his sweaty, grubby little hand, consequently melting the now squashed offering, the poor unsuspecting runner would grab at the melted chocolate gloop and spend the next part of the run trying to get to the water station to wash the whole sticky mess off. My mum had told me not to take sweets from strange men, she didn't say anything about over-excited children.

After about 18 miles, my already slowed-down pace decreased in speed, my nipples hurt and my shoelace was coming undone. I was, in fact, coming apart at the seams.

I had already decided that, no matter what, I would not walk, I would run the whole marathon. Consequently, I chose to ignore the now rapidly unravelling shoelace and I discovered that I could alleviate the pain in my oh so tenderised nipples whilst on the move by simply hooking my thumbs through my vest shoulder straps and pulling the fabric away from my now bleeding nipples. Pleased with my improvised nipple protection device, I could once again concentrate on the job in hand, reaching the finishing line.

I eventually reached the 20 mile mark, this was a huge psychological boost, if I could just hold on a little while longer, just another six miles, I would be a marathon runner. However, the fact that my shoe was now turning into a flipflop meant that I had no choice but to stop and re-tie the offending lace.

I eased my way over to find a parking space, bent over and suddenly realised that the once simple act of doing my shoelaces up had now become a major challenge. I had to inch my way down on knackered, painful legs, re-tie the laces with sweaty, shaking hands and then slowly, very slowly, inch my way back up to the upright position. Once that was done, I had to somehow work out a way to resume forward momentum. Looking and feeling like Frankenstein's monster, I dragged one stiff, rapidly cramping leg in front of the other – it took half a dozen zombie-like steps before I resumed anything like a plod.

It was now that I really appreciated the crowds of supporters. They shouted words of encouragement, willing me and every other runner to carry on. I'm sure that had I been left alone to sort myself out, I would have had a little rest, sat there and, in all probability, seized up and cried!

Carrying on like some fully paid-up member of the Ministry of Very Silly Walks, I managed to reach the Embankment. The supporters were so numerous that it was only very occasionally that you actually caught a glimpse of the River Thames, but the sheer noise of thousands upon thousands of cheering, clapping people sort of carried you along.

The crowds were so vast that you really could not see anything of this part of London, just corridors of people, whose enthusiasm was infectious. They certainly helped me to keep going.

I plodded along, soaking up the atmosphere, appreciating every single clap and cheer. I might have been getting slower, but at least I was inching my way closer to the finish line.

Turning onto Birdcage Walk and the crowds were unbelievably more densely-packed than before. I smiled and realised that I was close to the finish, which I seemed to remember was somewhere in front of Buckingham Palace.

At last, I saw the 26 mile marker, it was only then that I remembered a small but somewhat significant fact. The marathon, as anyone who has ever run one will tell you, is actually 26.2 miles long, the last point 2 was going to hurt.

Taking a right-hand turn, I could now see Buckingham Palace on my left as well as the Victoria Memorial, ergo the finish. I tried to speed up, creeping ever closer – wrong, it was only when I reached the memorial that I realised that another right-hand turn took me onto the Mall and the ever-elusive finish line was much further along.

The crowds and the noise were deafening, the power and enthusiasm displayed by the supporters quite literally pushed you along. With just a few yards to go, I made a feeble attempt to speed up, more for show than anything. I crossed the finish line and the large overhead clock announced to the world that I had taken 4 hours 7 minutes and a few seconds. With the 11 minute deduction (time it took to get to the start line) the actual time was a very pleasing 3 hours 56 minutes.

Immediately after the race, I collected my goody bag, kit bag and the most important thing of all – my Finishers medal.

I also spent the next couple of days wearing plasters on my nipples and walking down the stairs backwards!

I went on to complete the London Marathon 4 times; 1997, 1998, 1999 and 2004.

The Runner's Nuts

Chapter 7
Training

Train little, hard and often'
Jim Peters (Marathon Runner)

Training is one of the necessities of any runner's life and, just like your choice of training shoe, how you train is personal. What works for me might not work for you and vice versa. What works for you, won't work for me.

The Australian athlete, **Herb Elliot, one of the greatest ever middle-distance runners and multi world record holder seems to confirm that training is indeed a very personal, individual thing when he says, *"The more I speak to athletes, the more convinced I become that the method of training is relatively unimportant. There are many ways to the top and the training method you choose is just the one that suits you best. No, the important thing is the attitude of the athlete, the desire."*

I'm far from qualified to go on about the various training regimes, the rights and wrongs of various 'must do' exercises.

*Jim Peters. Born: 1918-1999. Broke the marathon world record 4 times and was the first person to ever do a sub 2:20 marathon.

**Herb Elliot. Born: 1938- Is still considered by many to be the greatest distance runner of all time. He held the mile record of 3:54.5 and ran sub 4 minute miles 17 times. Held the record for 1500 meters at 3:36 and only ever lost at that distance once.

When I first started training for Ultras it was (and still is) all very hit and miss, trial and error and much like I race. I bumbled along until I achieved the goal I wanted. In 1994 the sport of Ultra distance running was such that it was difficult, if not impossible, to find any information. Training for ultras has in itself become big business. Runners and ex-runners, can and do charge people an absolute fortune, which is fine for those people with a small fortune to spend. There is now a huge market for books, magazines, training camps, online experts and seminars, etc.

The trouble with any type of training programme is simple, you are not buying a guaranteed finish. The greatest runner/teacher in the world can come up with the best training programme, a bespoke programme tailor made to suit you, a programme that even if you managed to follow it diligently and to the letter, can't help with the most important part of completing such an extreme challenge, the mental side, the determination, desire and perseverance required to reach the elusive finish line. That is something that comes from within, you can't buy desire and desire to complete an extreme race is the one thing that you must have and must supply yourself.

In 2013, I was one of only four people to have completed a 352 mile race in the Arctic. The 6633 Ultra is a notoriously tough and unforgiving race, so much so, that at the time of writing only 11 people had managed to reach the finish line. The 6633 was familiar to me because I had attempted it some five years earlier and I had failed miserably. It was my first DNF (did not finish) in 12 years of racing the toughest races that I could find.

My reasons for my DNF in that particular race were many. The official reason was that I had injured my back- it wasn't an accidental injury, it was an injury that could have so easily been avoided. Owing to my cockiness, lack of preparation, research and/or getting my rather lofty ambitions mixed up with my equally limited abilities, saw my equipment fail spectacularly. Rather than fix the problem I chose to ignore it, a consequence of which saw me injure myself. Had I have done the necessary research, which incidentally is another very important aspect of training, I could have avoided the equipment failure and thence the injury. The point I'm trying to make is that training the body is one thing, doing homework and research is another, as is visualisation – bear with me.

Visualisation is just a fancy way of saying thinking things through, having a mental image of what lies ahead, things like, what type of terrain is likely to be encountered, how I'm going to be feeling, particularly when tired, problems that may need to be resolved, ie equipment failure, navigation, fatigue, nutrition or injury. I try to think about the possible worst case scenarios: getting lost, equipment breakage etc and how I am going to resolve or repair a problem? It's Sod's law that the problem will only occur when you are tired, pissed off or both. You need to have the answers ready, not stand around at 3:00 in the morning, in temperatures of minus whatever, wasting precious moments trying to figure out what to do next. have enough trouble trying to decide whether or not to have a wee, let alone having to start working out some complicated problem solving puzzle.

An example of this forward planning was mentioned in my last book, 'Fartleks and Flatulence'.

One of my poles broke, (the aluminium pole that connects my harness to the sled) Luckily for me it was a break that I had seen happen to someone before-they had been using an identical sledge so I had worked out how to fix it should the same thing happen to me. That bit of pre-planning would now pay dividends, a Leatherman™® multi tool, jubilee clip and a short screw were already in my pocket and, in less than five minutes, the repair had been made.

I can assure you that had I not been prepared, it would have taken a whole lot longer just to find the necessary bits required to fix the thing, let alone try and work out how to fix it. I would, in all probability, have just got my sleeping bag out, got some sleep and then sorted it out later when I woke.

When I first started racing in the Arctic (or any kind of environment) I took far too much kit. A 'just in case' mentality had set in. Arriving back home, I simply unpacked the unused kit that had been packed nearly a month earlier, kit that I had lugged around with me, 'just in case.' It took a few races to finally build up enough courage/confidence to leave behind a large amount of the 'just in case' kit. In other words, experience had given me the knowledge and confidence to pare my kit down.

Research, homework and visualisation are parts of training required – so easy but nonetheless important.

Physical Training

The physical training, however, requires discipline, ability to get out and run/train when time is tight and the weather is shite. Your mates want to go out and home life is not right. You seem to have loads of time before the actual race, you ache and hurt after the last session, your favourite team is in the final, it's the kids' birthday, you really need to do that course that the boss has lined up for you, the list for not training is endless. I'm fortunate that I'm very poor, vain and cowardly. Basically, I don't want to die and I most certainly don't want to look stupid, also, I have to finish because I couldn't afford to go back and try again and I haven't got the balls to return home and say to Mrs Berridge I didn't finish. She would no doubt tell me I could have put the money to better use. For me these are good enough reasons to get off my arse and train. The reality is that there are days when I would sooner not train, when it's a major pain in the arse to even put my training shoes on but, fortunately, I have now done enough races to know better.

I also try to add variety, simply to add interest and stave off the monotony of long, lonely plodding hours of running. Things like Adventure races, Triathlons and fun events like the famous Tough Guy (see the chapter on 'Tough Guy') all add an interesting and, for me, non-competitive element to training.

I don't normally wear a watch whilst training: both the timing and speed of a training run are irrelevant. For me it's all about distance and quality, so what if I happen to be 3 minutes slower on a ten mile run than I was last time I did that same run? I try to bank the miles, not the time. I run how I feel, not what the watch tells me to run, I listen to my body, sometimes I fly round and sometimes I plod round. However, having said that, there are occasions when my ego takes over. If I see someone running up ahead, I will, for some bizarre reason try to catch them, likewise if I happen to see someone running behind me, I will speed up in the hope that they can't catch me. I'm afraid that it doesn't only apply to other runners, I apply the same odd behaviour to mountain bikers, walkers and horse riders. The male ego has a lot to answer for.

I don't bother counting the miles and I certainly don't eat sensibly, I have a sweet tooth that needs satisfying and I much prefer to keep what little willpower I do possess for the race and not use it up denying myself that extra helping of sticky toffee pudding! I truly believe that you don't have to live like a monk or become a slave to what, is after all, supposed to be a fun hobby. Having said that, I'm only talking from the perspective of a bloke that only ever trains to reach the finish line, to be a Über competitive racing snake, well, that's a whole different ballgame.

Another thing that I consider important (for me personally) is that I always train on my own. There is only me, no one to push me, if I want to run slow I will, likewise if I feel good and decide to push the pace I will. I can do either without feeling obligated to anyone else. Another important reason for the solitary training is the simple fact that, during the race, especially 100 mile plus races, there is a very good chance that you will find yourself on your own for a very long time. I've done races where I have not seen another human being for two or three days. Being on my own doesn't phase me, I'm not, by nature, a person who enjoys monk-like solitude but I do both enjoy and savour the solitude.

Author and coach Roy Benson noted that *"Mentally tough runners have the discipline to not race in practice in order to win workouts. They can control their urges to run fast at the beginning of workouts or races when running feels easy and will not give in to the temptation to slow down when the inevitable fatigue sets in over the last one-third to one half of the workout or race"* In other words, have the balls or discipline to do your own thing and do not follow the crowd.

Because so many people have, over the years asked me about my training for Ultras, I decided that for my participation in the 6633 Ultra (see www.6633ultra.com) I would keep a record of my training, something that I have never done before. My training for this tough 352 mile Arctic race really started with a leisurely North Downs Way 50 miler in the August before the race in the following March. This NDW 50 was a race that I wouldn't be racing, I would use it as my first training session. Consequently I had to curb my enthusiasm, finishing in a time of 10.37, I had felt comfortable throughout, no aches or pains. The day after, I ran a steady 6.8 miles. The fact that I run the day after a race is a habit I developed years ago. What ever race I do (the smallest is 10 miles) I always make sure I run the next day, even for marathons. As I have already mentioned, I also take part in what I call novelty, fun races, things like the infamous Tough Guy, Triathlons and Adventure races, these add variety.

After the NDW 50, there was a slow, steady buildup of miles of 40/50miles per week during September. Then, from October, my semi-structured proper training began. I would love to impress you with an amazingly well-structured, seemingly professional approach but nothing could be further from the reality. Please don't expect a wonderfully scientific, calorie- counting, number crunching, time-orientated approach. Like my racing and writing, it is amateurish and unscientific, but it works for me.

I train roughly 8 days out of ten, though I do cycle the 10.1 miles to work ie: a little over 20 mile daily commute. I have a small gym at home, that over the years, I have managed to build up. Don't get the Idea that I'm a very rich person or one that has more money than sense. It's taken 18 years buying one item at a time and now I have a treadmill, nordic xc ski machine, rowing machine, all bought on finance one at a time, some weights and a Swiss ball.

Two Weeks in Snowdonia

October was a great time for me to knuckle down with training. Five months before the race allowed for enough time for a steady build up and for the first two weeks of October we had booked a cottage in Snowdonia for a two week holiday.

I am the first to admit that I am the worlds luckiest man: my wife has always supported my Ultra running aspirations (she once said that she would sooner I was an Ultra runner than a golfer!) and, luckily for me she has herself run numerous marathons, half-marathons and a couple of Ultras – the Atacama Crossing and the Namib Desert Challenge. Our two week holiday was on the understanding that I could train and faff about until noon each day. After that, I was warned that we were on holiday.

My wife and I arrived at the cottage that we had rented for the fortnight on the Friday evening. We spent Saturday leisurely walking around, drinking coffee and eating cake,(I think I have already mentioned the sweet tooth) whilst familiarising ourselves with the immediate area. We have been to Snowdonia on numerous occasions, so know the area well, but the secluded valley that we were in, was exactly that, secluded, beautiful and wild with some fantastic walks/runs.

Sunday 14/10/12

07:00 Out into a soggy, wet Welsh morning. The ground was boggy and hilly, and the inconsiderate Welsh sheep had churned up large areas of what was supposed to be a path, my shoes not only made that annoying squelching, sucking noise but they also collected great clods of wet mud. My super-dooper Salomon™® Speed cross GTX training shoes were rendered useless – with so much mud attached to each shoe traction was non-existent and the deep puddles just filled the shoes with dank, stagnant soup-like water.

Once the path petered out, the incline got a little more noticeable until I reached an abandoned old slate quarry, then the climbing got both technical and severe. Once I reached the top, I turned round and headed for home. The return trip was a lot more testing, the downhill required skill and concentration: wet, slippery and very loose underfoot. I loved it. A total distance of 18km, not huge but it was a tough run, reflected in a time of 2 hours 13 minutes. I was pleased, and I had felt good throughout.

Monday 15/10/12

Today I would run up to the summit of Snowdon, via the Rhyd-Ddu path. Unfortunately, it was pissing down, sorry, there was heavy precipitation. I sat in the car park, trying to make a decision, whether or not I should go up or go back. It was bad enough down here in the car park and looking up at to where I thought the summit should be, all I could see was dark fast-moving, angry-looking clouds. Then I remembered that I had spent a small fortune on Haglofs™® waterproof kit. Decision made, I got out of the car and got kitted up, if nothing else, I thought, I looked the part – shame all the sensible people stayed in and were thus unable to appreciate my new Haglofs™®.

Leaving the warmth and relative comfort of the car, I made my to the start of the path. Crossing the railway line, I couldn't resist another quick peek at the summit, still nothing, except the still fast-moving, dark, menacing clouds. Employing a mixture of walking and running, I made good and comfortable progress. The effort required soon had me nice and warm. Passing through another gate, and with the wind blowing hard, it was with my heart in my mouth that I made my way along a very steep section, Blwch Main, so steep and sheer was the drop on my left that my right hand instinctively reached for the wall to my side. With the wind gusting and buffeting me, desperately trying to remove me from the mountain, the clouds parted just long enough for me to catch a glimpse of my target – the Snowdon summit cafe. Unfortunately, it was at this point that my cowardly-custard gene kicked in and advised me in no uncertain terms that it was time to turn around. I couldn't really argue common sense had, on this occasion overridden macho pride. It was tricky trying to turn around and I had to watch each and every step. Once I was back on the Llechog Ridge, I could start running again. Back in the car park, I looked at my watch, 2 hours 8 minutes. I was pleased with the time. Even though I hadn't reached the summit, I was bloody close, maybe half a mile away, roughly 7 miles and in those conditions, I knew that it was beyond my ability to keep going, if only because I wanted to live long enough to do the 6633 Ultra.

Tuesday 16/10/12

An easy run today, 13.5km on an undulating country road, raining and windy, and relatively straightforward. Feeling good, I was able to push the pace a bit, finishing in a time of 1 hour 11 minutes.

Wednesday 17/10/12

Today's run was once again to the summit of Mount Snowdon. This time, however, I would be going up the easier most popular route, the Llanberis path. The weather was again crap: windy and raining and again looking up at where the summit should have been there was nothing but those same dark, angry, fast-moving clouds.

Leaving Llanberis and onto the Llanberis path, the initial early parts were, and indeed, are extremely steep. Discipline and a sensible pace early on were essential, lest I end up too bloody knackered. As it was, I was soon hot and breathing hard. Once the early, steep bits were out of the way and I was on the path proper, I could settle into a nice steady (for steady read slow) pace. I know this path well and knew how to pace it, I had already decided that, no matter what, I would run the whole lot – failure to do so would mean that I could not go into the famous Pete's Eats ("Probably the best cafe in the world", The Guardian 1988) for a big plate of something delicious, a mug of tea and probably a big bit of cake. Even this early on, it was proving to be a tall order, with the wind trying to keep me from moving forward. I did what I am good at and slowed down. I pushed rather than ran my way forward. It was head down, slow cautious running, passing under the small railway bridge and the path became a little more exposed. Wind gusts blew me off-balance a couple of times and trying to run with buttock-clenching fear was not easy. It was with great relief that I reached the familiar finger of rock that indicated I was very nearly there, about a 100 metres to go or should I say that I was nearly at the halfway point ie. the summit. Once the summit cairn was reached, I turned around and made my way down. Caution was the key word. Once on the bottom, I checked my time – 2 hours 57 minutes I was pleased, that I had run most of it, but just not enough to deserve a Pete's Eats treat.

Thursday 18/10/12

Another easy running day and a repeat of Tuesday's run, a 13.5km run on the same undulating country road, slightly slower with a time of 1 hour 13 minutes. With that, my training for the day was done – even though my wife had said that I could train until 12:00, the short road runs only took an hour or so, with the training over with so quickly, we could spend the rest of the day on holiday, like normal people.

The point I'm trying to make is that training whilst on holiday need not be all time-consuming and become so invasive that it encroaches or impacts. If you can compromise and be sensible, it should avoid resentment and those super, short road running days had the added bonus of scoring Brownie points – never a bad thing!

Friday 19/10/12

Today was a combination of running and walking. Again, I didn't need the 12:00 deadline as we would both be running/walking together. It's just nice to go out with my wife, her gentler more sensible approach does me the world of good and keeps me in check. We had looked at the maps, picked a waterfall that we would both like to see and off we went. The route was hilly and technical but great fun.

A total distance of 22km.

Saturday 20/10/12

Today, I would once again climb to the summit of Snowdon, this time, however, a walk up the Llanberis path with my wife. The weather for the moment was good, but again looking up at the summit, it didn't look so good up there: ominous, dark, menacing clouds. Walking up at a fairly brisk pace, we had passed several people before we had reached the halfway cafe. Passing the cafe, we again saw a few walkers and soon caught and passed them. We reached the summit cafe and had a leisurely coffee before making the return journey.

A distance of about 15 km in a little over 3 hours 20 minutes.

Sunday 21/10/12

A repeat of the route I had done on day one, only this time, instead of turning around once, I hit the top of the disused slate quarry. I carried on and onto a path, through a stile and dropped down into some woods. I felt good running at a nice steady pace, eventually reaching a bench that overlooked the stunning view. Using this as a marker, I turned around for the return journey and climbed out of the woods, back into the quarry and home. Legs felt good and I was able to pick up the pace a bit.

Total time of 3 hours 47 minutes.

Monday 22/10/12

Small 13.5 km road run at a leisurely pace, 1 hour 19 minutes.

Tuesday 23/10/12

I managed to sneak two runs in today whilst the boss went shopping!). Undulating 13.5 km road run with a 30 minute break separating them, 1 hour 14 minutes and 1 hour 17 minutes. Felt good, but the legs know that they have been busy.

Wednesday 24/10/12

Another trip to the slate quarry, a tough 18km and a time little over 2 hours 20 minutes. Though my speed seemed to be decreasing, it didn't bother me. I wasn't concerned, it was the accumulation of quality miles. Roughly 115 good quality, hilly, challenging miles in the two weeks plus dog walking and the hills that I was banking on, building up strength, endurance and confidence over rough terrain.

After Wales.

Those 2 weeks of good quality training and holiday show that training whilst on holiday need not be all time consuming. It's so important that this most selfish of sports/hobby, namely Ultra distance running, does not allow you to become so self-absorbed that you end up excluding or not considering the non-running partner. On the one hand Ultra distance running is a solitary, even insular sport If you are not training for Ultras, you are normally thinking about Ultras, however, I have learned that this solitary sport must also be a team sport and by that I mean that it is important to train and race around your family life, and not to have your family life evolve around your Ultra distance aspirations.

Sunday 28/10/12

A 6.8 mile, slow easy – run fairly flat.

Monday 29/10/12

Same 6.8 mile run, plus 2x 500 meters on the rowing machine, timed at 1 min 39 secs and 1min 42 secs.

Tuesday 30/10/12

Owing to the fact that I had a busy day at work, this was considered a rest day, though I did cycle the 20.2 miles to work and back.

Wednesday 31/10/12

A 9.3 mile hilly run, 20.2 mile cycle (to work and back) 1x 500 meter row at 1 min 41 secs, 50 abdominal crunches on the Swiss ball.

Thursday 1/11/12

20.2 mile bike, 9.3 mile hilly run, 1 mile treadmill run, incline level

15 (as steep as the machine will allow) at a time of 12min 57 secs, 500 meter row, 1min 44 secs. 60 abdominal crunches using the Swiss ball.

Friday 2/11/12

11.3 mile, slow run, hilly, 3 steep very long climbs, 500 meter row 1 min 44 secs, 2 hours later another run 6.8 miles, easy pace, immediately followed by a 1 mile run on the treadmill, incline 10, 11min 43 secs. 50 abdominal crunches followed by 60 crunches =110 crunches sets are roughly an hour apart.

Saturday 3/11/12

50 abdominal crunches, 11.3 mile slow hilly run, then, 500 meter row 1 min 39 secs, 2 hours later a 9.1 slow hilly run, immediately followed by 1 mile treadmill run, incline 15, 12 min 54 secs, 60 crunches, = 110.

Sunday 4/11/12

500 meter row, 1 min 47 secs, 9.1mile moderate pace hilly run, followed immediately by 1 mile treadmill run, incline 15, 12 min 54 secs, the 500 meter row at 1 min 41 secs. 50 abdominal crunches then 60 then 70 = 180.

Monday 5/11/12

500 meter row at 1 min 43 secs, 60 abdominal crunches, 9.3 mile hilly fast run, 500 meter row 1 min 46 secs, 70 crunches =130 and a 20.2 mile bike ride to work.

Tuesday 6/11/12

Run to work 10.1 miles 74 minutes (My wife picked me up)

Wednesday 7/11/12

Short day at work, finishing at 12.30 so cycled in and ran home, immediately got on the treadmill for the 1 mile uphill run, incline 15, time 13 min 7 secs.

Thursday 8/11/12

Day off work, went swimming just for fun (I hate swimming), cycled 5.3 miles to the pool, did 44 lengths and 3 times underwater widths. (I don't know why I mentioned that)

Friday 9/11/12

Ran 10.1 miles to work, cycled home.

Saturday 10/11/12

Cycle to work round trip of 20.2 miles I just noticed the date, ten, eleven, twelve, 10, 11, 12.

Sunday 11/11/12

Cycle to work, as above.

Monday 12/11/12

Short day at work, cycled in and home, 6.8 mile run, 1 mile treadmill run incline 15, 13 min 2 secs, 50 abdominal crunches.

Tuesday 13/11/12

Cycle to work and back 20.2 miles, 3.8 mile easy slow flat run, with my wife, 1 mile treadmill incline 15, 13 min 4 secs, 50 abs + 60 abs +50=160

Wednesday 14/11/12

10.1 mile cycle to work, 10.1 mile run home.

Thursday 15/11/12

No work. 500 meter row, 5 km ski machine (easy slow pace) 11.3 mile hilly slow run. 2 hours rest, 500 meter row, 9.1 mile slowish run with the occasional Fartlek, these are only done on the up hill sections (I'm slightly weird in that I actually enjoy running uphill). This run is again followed immediately by a 1 mile treadmill run on level 15 in a time of 13min 13 secs

Friday 16/11/12

9.3 mile hilly run, cycle to work and back 20.2 miles

Saturday 17/11/12

500 meter row leisurely 1.44, 5 km ski, leisurely, 11.7 mile slow hilly run. 2 hours later, 6.8 mile slow run, 500 meter row 1.47 followed immediately by a 1 mile treadmill run level 15 13 min 9 secs. I think I had better explain, lest you think I am the world's most selfish husband. My wife works most weekends, she has two types of shifts – an early shift, from 07:00 till 15:00 (That's when I do the training above) and a late shift from 15:00 to 23:00. As long as I manage to do various chores like the dishwasher, a quick hoover etc, it's usually left to the last minute, but I just about get away with it. I do try to train only when she is at work, sometimes we have a run together, which does me good because it keeps me in check and makes me run slower or, should I say run at a more sensible pace.

I work similar weird and wonderful hours, with shifts starting at 07:30 and finishing at 13:30 and shifts starting at 13:30 and finishing at 21:00. I do try and refrain from training when we both have a day off together. I'm not always successful but I try. Fortunately, I am a really annoying person to be around for too long, so if we have a few days off together, after about 3 days, my wife gets fed up with me and kicks me out so that she can have an hour's peace and quiet.

Sunday 18/11/12

12.4 mile slow, hilly run, 2 hours later, a 9.3 mile slow hilly run. 50 abs (swiss ball crunches) 60 abs, 70 abs, 80 abs, total=260, 1mile treadmill run level 10, 12mins 22 secs.

Monday 19/11/12

Cycle to work, hadn't got my cycling glasses on and a bit of something flew into my eye – bloody annoying, arrived at work looking like I had been crying. It did remind me of earlier in the summer when I was cycling to work and a wasp flew into my helmet, I don't know who panicked more, me or the wasp. I had to stop and remove the frantic thing, because, I can assure you, that there is nothing very pleasant about having a wasp in your helmet!

Run home

Tuesday 20/11/12

Run to work, cycle home.

This format varies very little, however, it peaks out at around weeks 6, 7, and 8 prior to the race, those 3 weeks are the highest mileage (also should I trip, pull something or suffer an injury, I have enough time to recover). If I left my high mileage sessions nearer to the race, I might not have enough time, well that's the theory ie. my big run now becomes 17.4 miles followed 9.7 then the miles on incline 15 always attempting a time of between 12 mins and 12 mins 10 secs.

Uniquely, I incorporated the age old, tried and tested, tyre-pulling training in preparation for the 6633 Ultra, this type of training isn't normal practice but I learned the hard way. The 6633 wasn't a normal race, I only pulled the rather large tyre for a couple of miles at a time but they were hilly miles and I only did 23 sets, over a 4 month period. Six weeks prior to the race. I start a very slow taper.

Another little trick I use whilst on the treadmill is to run the first half a mile with my hands clasped behind my back – this causes me to rely on pure legwork, which makes me run far harder. The body's natural running style is to make use of the arms to pump/propel the body forward: without the use of my arms, the 12 minute run becomes a bloody efficient workout! (I did tell you that I am slightly different!!).

When I do have a couple of non-running days, I try to incorporate some weight-training. Again, there is no real structure to my so-called weight-training. I do light weights but a lot of reps.* The same as I do with the abdominal crunches, not one huge number but loads of small sets.

The weights I use are just 10 kilos, I start with 10 arm curls,** then every so often I do another set, increasing the amount by five, until I reach 50. At the same time that I am doing a set of curls, I will do a set of abs, so the arm curls will be 10, 15, 20 etc, the abs will be 20, 30, 40 etc, until I reach the 100. The number of reps are not terrifically high but the accumulation of numbers is, for me, very effective.

Another thing that I have built into my training plan is what I call a 'shit or bust' day, the scientific or clever academic types would probably call this a training day, something really impressive like lactate threshold or anaerobic training. To me, this is just a tough day, 'shit or bust', balls to the wall day, when I push as hard as I possibly can, I push myself to my absolute limit. On this day, I do three runs, the 11.1 mile run incorporates a couple of stiff climbs, from my house to the Tennyson Monument here on the Isle of Wight. A long, challenging assent to the top at 147 meters or 482ft then back down to sea level and onto the Freshwater Bay Golf Course at a similar height and equally challenging. 2 hours after that run I do the 9.3 mile run, again incorporating a couple of steep hills including the golf course and immediately after that run a 1 mile treadmill run on incline 15. Those three runs are done at my limit, again, I don't time them but I do push them and I am usually shaking and crying – well maybe not crying, by the time its over. Fortunately, I only do that in a lead up to a race and at least 6 weeks prior to race day. Because my normal training is not timed or pushed too hard, I occasionally need to see what my physical limit is and know the warning signs of my physical limit. I know, weird!

As you can see, there is nothing remotely scientific, nothing is really timed, I train when and how I feel. I am, however, disciplined enough to get off my arse and put the work in (as I mentioned earlier, being a vain coward helps).

I'll try to explain my reasoning for the type of training I do.

The reason that I run two or three times a day is to sort of replicate race conditions. During a race, you arrive at a checkpoint, stop for a short period and then have to get yourself going again. If my body was used to only ever doing one run a day, every time I stopped for any length of time it would assume that it had finished being active for the day and automatically start to shut down, switch off, stiffen up and start the recovery/repair process. I also believe that if I was knocking out the 20, 25, 30 mile plus, single runs my very old body would start to rebel, bits would fall off, seize up, struggle and rebel. I would, in effect, be more prone to injury.

Even when I haven't a race planned or the next race is many months away, I still run 30/35 miles a week, still cycle to and from work, do a few abs and faff about on the rowing machine. All this is done as and when I feel like it and if and when time permits, but I always try my best to do a minimum of 3 of everything during the week, I also skip regularly, only five minutes at a time – on the patio and barefoot this seems to strengthen the knees, ankles etc. I train my body to recover quickly so that I can continue with the next section and the next. I also try not to mix my sports, I remember years ago training for the London Marathon. Three weeks before the marathon, we went out and played Ten Pin Bowling, my legs and hips were in bits the next day. I tried volleyball and again I was in bits, so I leave well alone now.

My little and often approach works for me and has done for nearly 20 years. I've never got stressed about training times or reaching targets and nutrition. It's all about when and how I feel, I eat what I like. Consequently, I have not only remained injury-free but also still enjoy training and racing and that, I am afraid, is what it has always been about: ENJOYMENT!

*Repetitions

Nutrition

This is another one of those areas that, like my physical training, is made up and personalised to suit me and I suppose that, because I'm allegedly an Ultra Distance Athlete I have mastered the art of sports nutrition, nothing could be further from the truth. For a start, I don't eat breakfast, I make do with cups of tea or real ground coffee. The perceived wisdom is that breakfast is the most important meal of the day, I never fancy eating at that time of day, so I don't bother. To add to my rather weird eating habits, I eat just once a day, no lunch or snacking, but a really good evening meal and lots of it. This eating once a day all started back in the 80s when I worked on a piecework system, this piecework meant that I got paid for what I produced. I developed a knack for working long nonstop hours without the need for stopping for anything, including food.

I can train and go to work without eating a thing until the evening, the only downside is that I then eat like a horse.

With the benefit of hindsight, piecework was a great grounding for Ultra distance running, I learned to work for a very long time without eating or stopping.

With regard to what I eat, I subscribe to Arthur Newtons* theory that says *"The only definite dietary rule that can be laid down for all and sundry would be 'eat what you like'. Nature generally knows what is needed is right. Satisfy your digestion with anything that you seem to fancy and you need have no qualms."*

I eat healthy meals, but do have a sweet tooth that needs satisfying. I like chocolate, cakes and puddings. What little determination I do possess is reserved for getting off my arse and going training.

Not denying myself cakes and chocolates.

When I do train or race, my body seems go through phases of craving certain foodstuffs, ie. salt or sugar. I get the sudden urge to have crisps or chocolate, so much so that during multi-day Arctic races, I have savoury food in all my pockets on my right-hand side and sweet food in the pockets on the left. These cravings seem to confirm that Arthur Newton was right, eat what the hell you like, your body knows best.

I would sooner eat four bars of chocolate and two tubes of Pringles™® crisps during a race than what some nutritionist says is the recommended protein/carbohydrate ratio. Get any food down that you can stomach rather than try and force down something that you and your body really doesn't want but that the expert's advice.

Incidentally or coincidentally, my weight has remained the same for the whole time that I have been racing. Every medical I have ever had (and they are usually compulsory for an Ultra Race) has confirmed my weight as being 12st 7lbs or, for you youngsters, 79.378 kgs

*Arthur Newton. 1949

The late great Arthur 'Greatheart' Newton 1883-1959 is arguably the greatest long distance runner of all time, multi world record holder and multi Comrades Ultra Marathon winner.

Rowing my lawn

Training in the garden

Chapter 8
What it takes!

What does it take to compete and
complete an Ultra Distance race?

Ultra distance endurance running is a very strange sport, taken in part, it could be argued, by very strange people.

Initially, when I started training for that very first race, the 1996 Marathon Des Sables, my total ignorance and absolute naivety had led me to believe that physical fitness was the key. I would need to be extremely fit to run such an extreme race. After all, I reasoned, runners need to be fit and marathon runners need to be extremely fit, if only because the marathon is a very long race. Ergo, the longer the race the fitter you need to be.

However, it took me less than one race to realise that that simple theory was deeply flawed.

Contrary to what anyone may think, Ultra distance running is not just a physical sport, it is predominantly a mental challenge and my personal experience would seem to suggest that it is, at the very least, 70% mental and probably nearer 80%.

The Marathon Monks of Japan who, in order to qualify for a mind-blowing 1000 days of mountain marathon running, must first master the art of seated meditation. More emphasis is placed on meditation than is placed on physical ability/fitness. These Marathon Monks study a form of Buddhism known as Tendai and, to attain a higher level of spirituality, they push their bodies to the absolute limits of physical endurance, spending seven years running 1000 marathons on Mount Hiei, a mountain just North East of the city of Kyoto, the ancient capital of Japan. In the first year, the Marathon Monk will complete the 26.2 miles for 100 consecutive days, the second year, third and fourth years will see the monk repeating the 100 days of consecutive marathons and then, unbelievably, it starts to get difficult. Year five and the monk will complete 100 days of marathons TWICE!

On the 700th day, they will start 9 days of fasting. No food, no water, no resting and no sleeping, then and only then will they be allowed to proceed.

The 6th year will consist of 100 days of consecutive 37.5 mile marathons and only once that has been achieved, will the Monk reach the seventh and final year, which will include 100 days of 52.2 mile marathons before finally tapering off, which consists of a further 100 days of normal 26.2 marathons.

It's hard to imagine that this almost superhuman feat is taken on, not for cash, pride, ego or praise – it's done because the Mountain Monk wants simply to achieve Spiritual Enlightenment. Mental tenacity and sheer willpower to achieve what most normal people would call the unachievable.

Once they decide to take on this challenge, there is absolutely no chance whatsoever to not complete it, no chance to back out and have a rethink. Once they start, they must finish through bad weather, illness or even a change of heart because, should they not complete the challenge, they are duty-bound to commit suicide, either through ritual disembowelment or by hanging themselves with the belt from their robe, which I suppose is always a bit of an incentive to finish!

During my first race, the Marathon Des Sables, I was, along with the majority of the others, a complete and utter physical wreck. My decline was rapid – in less than three days, I was in tatters, I wasn't sleeping anywhere near enough, I wasn't able to eat enough to fuel my body for the enormous physical exertion I was demanding of it, I was drinking nowhere near enough and all that I was drinking was tepid bottle water that I was forced to carry in my hand. The water that I had occasionally quenched my thirst, however, the water alone was unable to supply the necessary electrolytes (in 1996 I had never heard of electrolytes, so was blissfully unaware of the fact that I was in all probability, depleting my body's levels of calcium, chloride, magnesium, phosphorous, potassium and sodium). On top of this my feet were shredded and swollen, so swollen that I had to do a bit of DIY surgery, by cutting away the loose, dead and blistered skin around my heals and by removing the insoles, for insoles read 'cushioning.' I was able to squeeze my oversized, swollen feet into my now very undersized shoes. My rucksack, that weighed some 13 kgs (28 lbs) was too heavy and bloody uncomfortable, the temperature was 120 degrees plus, I was worried about navigating and my nuts were being slowly and painfully chaffed. But. every day, I got up and slowly pushed on and plodded away until I reached the elusive finish line.

I know it's mental drive but where does that drive come from? When every ounce of your being is telling you to stop, why don't you? When every piece of logic and common sense is saying enough, time to call it a day, when you know the only way for the pain to stop is to actually stop, such a simple act that solves everything.

During that first race, there were proper runners and athletes. Extremely fit people, people that had completed triathlons, marathons, fell runners and military personnel to name but a few and yet some of them never made it to the finishing line. Why?

I was just a bloke who hadn't run since school, was rapidly approaching middle age, had spent the weeks leading up to and including the race in a perpetual state of fear. I was tattered and torn, sleep-deprived, dehydrated and undernourished but I had somehow completed what I had set out to achieve, while many others didn't.

It's a question that fascinates me and, even after all this time and with all the races that I have done, it remains a question to which i don't know the answer.

One of my favourite quotes that seems to confirm the need for mental tenacity over physical ability is by Apsley Cherry-Garrard in his book 'The worst journey in the world.' He says "It is not by strength of body but rather strength of will which carries a man farthest where mind and body are taxed at the same time to their utmost limit."

Another great, very simple little quote that seems to sum up the fact that it is willpower over physical ability is by Victor Hugo. He says "People do not lack strength, they lack will."

An absolute and essential prerequisite, will power, mental drive, stubbornness or determination, whatever you may call it – it is far more important than physical fitness/ability and yet, unlike physical fitness, it can't be trained.

In the book 'The Worlds Toughest Endurance Challenges' by Richard Hoad and Paul Moore, I was asked the question,(about my finish in the 430 mile Yukon Arctic Ultra) "Why do some people fail to finish and others don't?" I replied, "Ego, pride, stubbornness, vanity". I still don't know the answer. In the end, I had simply wanted, no, had to reach Dawson – absolutely nothing else mattered.

After my first DNF (Did not finish) during the 2008, 6633 Ultra, I wasn't sad or depressed and the reason for my lack of sadness was simple: I had no choice and there it is in a nutshell -choice, you choose to go on or you choose to stop. Had I had the luxury of choice, I would, in all probability have made the wrong one, either I carried on and risk permanent or serious injury (I had injured my back pulling a broken sledge) or I stop and spend the rest of the time thinking I should have and I could have carried on! I went to finish that race some five years later.

Choice, you have to really want that finish line. Put simply, if your legs say enough, no more, it hurts, your mind has the ability to override them. However, if your mind says the same, your legs have no chance, the mind can push the body, but the body cannot push the mind.

Fellow outdoor Enthusiast and Ultra Runner Tegyn Angel wrote the following article and it seems to capture the very essence of the Ultra Runner's mindset!

Darkness: How Ultra running can strip away our emotional barriers.

Deciding to run an Ultra for the first time is understandable. It's a big challenge. Whilst the personal reasons underlying the decision might not be readily apparent even to the runner, it's really not that difficult to communicate the essence of the challenge. To prove to ourselves, or others, that we have the fortitude to push through the limitations that we once imagined, defy the odds and endure hardship.

Once the challenge has been met, signing up a second time is a different matter entirely. The repeat offender is likely to have a predisposition to bingeing or addiction. While by no means an inviolate law, there's no question that a large number of our fellow Ultra runners have felt the symptoms of withdrawal and agitation after a big event. I find it unlikely that 10 to 20 hours of hormones coursing through our bodies leaves us with only doms to show for our efforts.

I love the feeling of strength, independence and fluid freedom I get from trail running and Ultras. Yet the more events I run, the more I come to fear the comedown. Knowing the Black Dog is waiting at the front gate for you is intimidating. Other than drugs and surrounding ourselves with loving distractions, often the only thing that helps us cope is going out for another run. Mind-boggling and incredibly frustrating for an injured runner.

I ran the Northburn100 a few months ago, a 100mile race in the mountains of New Zealand. It was tough. I crossed the finish line after 34hrs, physically fine but emotionally desolate. The RD calls it a "look of anguish". I'd say anguish is too energetic. Thinking back on Northburn, and other gruelling Ultras I've run, I've become increasingly aware that this post-event emotional rollercoaster is just as much a part of running Ultras as are the training, camaraderie, palate fatigue and physical endurance. Even when we smash the goals we set for ourselves, the feeling can be bittersweet.

It's exhausting work exploring the depths of our darkest emotions. When they're fresh, thoughts smash around our skulls like possessed plant equipment. We feel like there's a broken record playing up there, our thoughts playing some sick game of psychosomatic Hide and Seek with our clenched and twisted guts. Coming out of an Ultra, it's safe to say that we're fatigued. The exhaustion lingering from the event washes away our defences and this conscious scraping-back of the soul further erodes our reserves, allowing unbidden thoughts and feelings to threaten the already threadbare fabric of our sanity.

But what becomes of us if we shy away from the introspection? Does denial simply buy us time while these emotions ferment in our subconscious? Or am I being melodramatic? Maybe spending a day or two ignoring these things is just what they need — dismissal, pure and simple. Then again, perhaps the real benefit of endurance sport isn't physical, but spiritual; that enduring the ceremony and imbibing the potion of hormones our body releases puts us into a state so receptive to self-exploration that it would be damn near sacrilegious to ignore it. There's certainly been no shortage of writers, poets, artists and musicians who've found the Black Dog to be their greatest muse.

There are even a handful of groups around the peripheries of more mainstream cultures that have taken this metaphor literally. The Marathon Monks of Mount Hiei are known to seek enlightenment through extreme asceticism and physical endurance in running. In their quest for enlightenment, they will run 40km a day for 100days before requesting permission to continue their quest for another 900 days, the whole project taking them 7 years.

The Lung-Gom-Pa runners of Tibet likewise achieve enlightenment and a connection with God through running as a form of meditation. While the connection between physical and spiritual here is quite apparent, there are countless other cultures that extol the virtues of endurance, fortitude and a tolerance for both adversity and hardship. While these may seem physical in nature, they are most definitely spiritual.

Whilst I'm far too familiar with the darker end of our emotional spectrum to suggest that the Dog might be Man's Best Friend, rather than being a downside — something to fear and dread — perhaps the comedown should be appreciated, if not welcomed. As Kahlil Gibran wrote in The Prophet, "The deeper that Sorrow carves into your being, the More Joy you can contain."

By Tegyn Angel.

An article written by Tanya Basu again confirms that the sport of Ultra distance running is far more than a physical challenge.

The reason people run ridiculous distances has little to do with physical fitness.

The Ultra marathoner is a special sort of person. Generally, when people think about running and intensity, the two seem to follow a pretty correlated path: The more one runs, the more intense one must be. Running a 10K? pretty low-key. A half? Not too bad. A Marathon? Whoa, now we're getting to intense territory. And Ultra marathoners – those badass runners tackling distances that exceed the 26.2 of marathons, sometimes up to or more than 50 or 100 miles?

Clearly, Ultra marathoners are the most intense, gritty individuals.

What is the point, the uninitiated may wonder, of all that running? Whilst most people associate running with physical fitness, many Ultra marathoners argue that the reason that they run is not to get muscles or maintain cardiac health. Instead, it's to attain some sense of 'flow'- that nebulous term that's associated with that other very fuzzy concept that runners toss around 'Runners High.'

The Runner's Nuts

Chapter 9
Why on Earth!

Unfortunately for most Ultra distance runners, the three letter word beginning with 'w' that is most frequently used when we say to someone that we have just run an Ultra distance race is not WOW, it's WHY?

The most famous answer to that often-asked question is also the most accurate. "If you have to ask the question, you'll never understand the answer."

Why? Indeed! I have been racing Ultras long enough to now have a standard reply, which is usually "To see if I can," and "Because I want to." Unfortunately, the reality is somewhat different, especially when so many races that I have done have been my last. "Never again," seems to be a recurring theme – the amount of times that I have struggled to reach a checkpoint or a finish line. I'm usually in some degree of discomfort, hungry, sleep-deprived, chin-strapped, bolloxed or hanging out my hoop! I have vowed, promised and categorically stated that there is no way on God's green earth that I am ever putting myself through this again and then, rather annoyingly, I say the exact same thing during the next race!

When I took part in the 1996 'Marathon Des Sables,' I remember telling my wife that it was just a one-off, just one big adventure in my life, I've stopped telling my wife that the last race I did was my last or that the next race will be my last race.

I think it was Mark Twain that said, *"A classic is something that everybody wants to have read and nobody wants to read."* The Ultra is much like that, an Ultra is great to have done but quite literally a pain in the arse to do.

Why does anyone choose to push themselves to the extreme and not only choose to do it but pay good money to do it? I'm sure if you asked 10 ultra distance runners, "Why?" you would have at least ten different answers.

Do I feel the need to go back or do I just want to go back? I'm honestly not sure but I do know that there is no single easy answer as to why I want to take part in an Ultra extreme race. For me personally, it seems to be a small collection of answers and in no particular order. Because I want to, to see if I can, a love of exploring (seeing things during a race that most other people never get the chance to see) and travel. I need to push myself both physically and mentally, have a sense of achievement and a sense of well being, meeting great people from all over the world and from all walks of life, the list could go on. I also know that, for me where the race is, is just as important as what the race is.

I'm sure that most people who decide to take up that once-in-a-lifetime challenge, really mean it, however, I am also sure that those same once-in-a-lifetime people go on to do more than that one Ultra.

The American poet Diane Ackerman said, *"I don't want to get to the end of my life and find that I lived just the length of it, I want to have lived the width of it as well."*

Sir Adolphe Abrahams, who is considered by many to be the father of British Sports Science, put it more succinctly when he said in 1961 *"if any psychologist will take the trouble to trace out the history of each of our prominent pedestrians, he will discover that a very large proportion of them have been subject to some form of madness."* Whilst I agree that it takes a certain mindset to be able to push on through physical and mental limits, madness is a little strong, but then I would say that, wouldn't I?

Unfortunately, I'm no wordsmith. I have not the verbal skill or vocabulary to put into words the feeling of satisfaction, pride or sense of achievement that is experienced by someone that has pushed themselves to the absolute physical and mental limit, and very often beyond, to reach the finish line.

As you will see, after two decades of racing Ultras, I still haven't got a clue, got no idea why I, or indeed, we feel the urge to put ourselves through it. All I do know is that I love participating in them, taking on the challenge and having a bash – in fact I find it hard to understand why you wouldn't want to have a bash! I do know that, as long as my enthusiasm remains, I shall continue to do so.

Top Ten Reasons To do a Four Deserts Race.

Fellow Ultra Distance Runner and Gobi March competitor Penelope Boettiger came up with her top ten reasons, which seem to sum it all up rather nicely.

10: The Medal

Let's get this out of the way early. We all want the medal. It's big, its heavy, it's a symbol of all the pain and all the pride.

But there are better reasons to do a 'Four Deserts Race'

9: Food

Not during the actual event. There is nothing good to say about what you'll be eating during the event. But in the month following it? You can eat anything/everything you want and you still won't make up for all the weight that you lost during that week. In short, it's a free pass!

8: Get away from the kids

Usually you feel guilty when you are trying to duck the kids, but this is different. You are absolved of all child responsibility for the duration of the event (and travel…which can add days) by justifying it under the one banner.

The kids will reflect on this at some time in their lives, drawing on your mental and physical fortitude to overcome barriers in their own lives. (Look, we can't really test this theory out because they won't be grown up for years, so let's just assume it's true and move on)

7: Cool Injuries

What happened? Oh, I tripped over a sheep, slipped on the edge of a volcano, slipped into a rice paddy, was trying to avoid a camel…you just don't get cool injuries like this at home!

6: Your own kind of crazy

Everyone is crazy but with this group, you have a gathering of your specific kind of crazy. It's a nice change.

5: International Couch Surfing.

Forget Air BNB-you now have free places to stay all over the world, to go with your new friends from all over the world. Just keep that extra bed in your house ready-people are coming your way, too.

4: New Gear

Who doesn't love new gear? And who doesn't love getting to research and then purchase loads of new gear all at once, with absolutely no guilt whatsoever?! After all, you have to have … look at the mandatory kit list.

3: No Bathing or Shaving

Don't even bother to try to stay clean and fresh. You're going to smell like a wet dog, have blisters, furry legs, swollen ankles… and that's by day 2, embrace it. This is the chance of a lifetime, to walk around stinking and disgusting for a week or more and yet blend in with the other woolly forest creatures, sorry, I mean fellow competitors.

2: Try Out New Hairstyles

You know that style that you think would look great, but it's just a bit too edgy to take public? Well, this is your chance to wear that look and wear it proud!

1: Tan Lines

You just don't get tan lines like this at a beach resort. To those at home-strangers or not-who are familiar with taping, you look a badass. No lying around in a bikini for you last week. For those who look at your tan lines oddly and wonder what the *&^%$! Well, they aren't your kind of crazy, anyway.

So you want to run an Ultra.

Ultra running enthusiast, Taylor Fleishner, wrote the following top ten tips to help prepare for an Ultra distance race.

1: Be patient. Be patient with your training and be patient when racing. Start slow and do your own thing.

2: Choose a location you want to race in. A large part of the Ultra running culture is about running in places you'd never be able to see other wise – take advantage of it.

3: Build up your mileage slowly. If you overload yourself too quickly, it'll just lead to injury and then delay your training even further.

4: If you love the support you can have from family and friends during a race do your first race close to home. There are more great Ultras in the UK than ever before.

5: Get to know yourself and what you need to run your best. Once you've learned that, see if you can push yourself even further.

6: Put in the time you need to train properly. The culmination of those miles will be more meaningful than the race itself.

7: Runners love to talk. Go to your local running shop and ask questions and find fellow runners to aid in your training.

8: Walking training is just as necessary and important, especially for desert and races that involve climbing.

9: Always run your own race. Completing your first Ultra isn't about finishing first, it's about finishing.

10: Mostly, enjoy it! Running an Ultra is an incredible thing and an amazing achievement – one you'll never forget!

-Both those 'Top Tens' sum it up nicely – Penelope's 'Why the desire' and Taylor's What we require' explain the simple facts that humour and patience are key prerequisites for the aspiring Ultra Distance Runner!

Chapter 10
Physical Pain

Pain, much like your training shoes is an integral part of an Ultra distance runner's life, the one thing that is guaranteed about an Ultra distance race is the simple fact that it will hurt.

It's how you deal with the hurt that will undoubtedly dictate the outcome of your race.

I've been in races that have hurt and hurt a lot, things like chaffing and blisters are par for the course. I've even had frostbite and during a race called the 7x7x7 (7 marathons in 7 days, 7 different ways) I came off my mountain bike and broke my wrist. Unfortunately, I still had to row and kayak over 60 miles. Fortunately for me, however, I didn't know that I had broken the wrist – it bloody hurt and it was bloody uncomfortable but I continued until I achieved my goal of finishing the race, because, ultimately the hurt and the discomfort were just another minor inconvenience, another problem to overcome on my way to achieving my ultimate goal, finishing. Why! However, and rather interestingly, had I known that my wrist was broken I would not have continued: sometimes ignorance really is bliss.

I personally don't think that any race is worth long term serious injury. When I had frostbite on my feet, I took a gamble. It was a calculated gamble that I had weighed up very carefully. I knew that I could not under any circumstances allow my feet to get frostbitten or frozen for a second time, and had the frostbite occurred earlier on in the race, I am sure I would have pulled the plug and withdrawn (If that decision had not been made for me). It was only the fact that I was only 30 miles or so, approximately 18 hours from the finish line that made continuing a feasible, if slightly risky, option. I knew that I could protect and care for my feet for that last little bit of the race.

I don't know the physiology of pain but I understand the psychology and this understanding was learned the hard way during my very first race the 1996 'Marathon Des Sables.' During that race, what had once been my feet were replaced by raw, bloody stumps, the abrasive action of the very fine sand had sandpapered my feet into oblivion.

The agony when I wasn't using them was immense enough to try to put my full weight on them, by attempting to stand on them increased the agony. It was like standing on broken glass after they had been grated and then walking on red hot coals. Every step hurt, every time I kicked or scuffed a rock or stone a shot of nausea-inducing agony would shoot through my entire body, causing me to clench my fists and buttocks.

However, I realised that if I could just hang on long enough, if I could just man up and hobble, waddle, limp and somehow inch my way to the first checkpoint, the pain always seemed to lessen until, eventually, my feet became nothing more than just uncomfortable swollen shoe-fillers.

When any race starts getting painful (and it will somewhere along the line) I always have it in the back of my mind that the only way for me to STOP the pain is for me to reach the finish line. So, reaching the finish line becomes essential and nothing else matters

It appears to me that pain is there as a sort of built-in warning system. It warns you to stop whatever it is that you are doing, because whatever you are doing is going to cause damage- if you don't stop and you choose to ignore the warning, the damage will get worse.

However, it also seems to me that you can override the warning signals by ignoring them: this was borne out by the fact that, as each time I pushed on through the pain it lessened, it took a couple of hours of pure agony but eventually the pain receptors* got sick of telling me to stop and gave up sending signals.

Polar Explorer and Author, Dr Michael Stroud, says in his book "Survival of Fittest" that, *Evolution has fortunately designed the human body to ignore repetitive pain signals – a useful coping mechanism for the injuries of life."* Or Ultra distance running! Basically, man up, and tough it out!

Punishment Verses Pleasure

Hard physical labour, sleep deprivation and hours of solitary repetitive mind-numbing monotony – these three things are widely used and are very effective tools in both torture and punishment and yet the Ultra Distance Runner not only embraces them but pays for the pleasure. Why?

I remember the story of the man who used to bang his head against a wall for an hour a day and, when he was asked why he did it, he simply said, *"Because it feels so good when I stop."* I'm sure any Ultra distance runner understands that mans simple answer.

Short Term Memory

Another useful tool to possess is a short term memory. I have learned over the years that, no matter how much pain you are in (and somewhere along the line you will be), or how genuine the promise is of "Never, ever, doing anything so stupid ever again," during your lowest periods, of a race, you eventually forget.

This useful, forgetting ability was known by psychologists as 'Psychogenic Amnesia" – basically the brain is unwilling or unable to recall something that it considers to be stressful or too traumatic- a simple effective psychological defence mechanism.

When you are at home recounting the race to family and friends, you seem to forget the horrendous body odour problem, that no one else had noticed or had been too polite to mention. You forget the weeping blisters, diarrhoea, constipation, embarrassing chaffing, the fear of getting lost. You manage to convince yourself and your audience that it was a brilliant adventure, you try to explain the joy of hitting each checkpoint, the camaraderie, the sheer ecstasy of finally reaching the finish line and that it was really, worth every minute. In fact, you mention the fact that a few friends are planning to do another Ultra and you wouldn't mind joining them.

In effect, you remember the good, forget the bad and plan the next.

Chapter 11
How things have changed

In this, the age of instant communication and social media, things have become so much easier. Technology has allowed us, at the click of a button, to do many things. At the click of a button I can enter a race, pay for a race and research the race. I can even follow the race in 'real time.' Watch the race unfold before my eyes. I can send a message of support to a friend as they struggle from one checkpoint to the other. Likewise, I have received messages of support from home and been told what my position is within the race (I very often don't know) I have received news about friends who have dropped out, why they dropped and where they dropped. Of all of this, I am usually totally oblivious and yet, someone thousands of miles away knows more about what is going on in my race than I do.

When I first saw the Marathon Des Sables on 'Transworld Sport' I was so fascinated that I recorded it, it took a couple of minutes to find a video cassette tape (remember them) and then load the thing – nowadays I would just hit the record button without even leaving the comfort of my chair. However, had it not been for the Daily Telegraph newspaper doing a fairly in-depth piece on the race, it would just have remained a ten minute clip on video tape. I would not have had a clue of where or how to find out any details about the French race across the African Sahara. I read the article that was written by Mike Calvin and couldn't believe that those athletes were anything but superhuman. I found out that they weren't, they were me: ordinary, nondescript and average.

I figured that, as I more than qualify as being an ordinary, nondescript average person, I could also do the Marathon Des Sables. But how? It is a French race, held in Morocco across the Sahara Desert. There was no contact point in the article, no clue on the organisation behind it. I racked my brains (which didn't take long) and realised that the only way I would be able to find out about the race was to write to the journalist responsible for the article. I duly wrote the letter, walked to the postbox, posted the letter and prayed, that one, a busy journalist such as Mike Calvin would get my letter and two, if he did, he wouldn't think I was a weird time-wasting fantasist and throw the letter in the bin and three, he would take the time to sit and reply. He did reply and about three weeks later a letter from the Telegraph arrived. I read it, it gave me the name of the British organiser, I wrote a letter to the organiser and so the slow laborious pen to paper process started again. It took weeks just to find out how to enter that race.

Now ,however, when I see a race on the television, I can press the record button, run up stairs during the adverts, Google the race and print off the details all before the kettle has boiled, more information in 5 minutes than I had managed to glean in 5 weeks.

I can get the race website, e-mail a question and then once I have the information, I can do some homework ie: youtube the race, study the terrain, see what kit people are using, hear firsthand accounts, sign up to the newsletter and watch as the race unfolds and, if I decide to enter the race, I can pay for it instantly.

During my participation in the Yukon Arctic Ultra, part of the compulsory kit we were obliged to have was a SPOT TRACKER. This nifty little device would inform race HQ and anyone else with access to a computer exactly where I was, how fast I was moving and when I had stopped. It could also call for help or request an emergency rescue.

Friends and family can follow my progress from the comfort of home, contact the race HQ and send an e-mail, there is nothing better than to arrive at some really remote checkpoint in the middle of the Arctic or desert and be handed an e-mail from a loved one.

Another area that seen some amazing changes is kit. My first Ultra was the Marathon Des Sables, I spent as much time looking for kit good enough to survive 7 days of running through the desert as I did training. Eventually, and over a period of some months,

I had cobbled together an assortment of sorts. The rucksack was a small 35 litre day hiking pack, a pair of running shorts and socks, an ordinary off the shelf T-shirt, a pair of running shoes that just looked to be the most robust, a hat with matching fabric stitched onto the back to cover my neck and the biggest pair of sunglasses I could find. One of the reasons that I chose the rucksack was because it had pockets on the side, I thought that these pockets would come in handy for putting a bottle of water in. I was right, they did indeed allow me to put a bottle of water in, they just made it a pain in the arse to get the bottles in and out when I was moving, hence I had to carry a litre bottle in my hand during the whole race.

Looking on the MDS web site recently I noticed a whole load of branded kit designed specifically for the Marathon Des Sables, a super lightweight 590g ruck sack with storage in the front for easy on the move access, a built-in rain cover, poncho, flask carriers, hydration bag with drinking straw, sleeping mat and even an MP3 player holder. Gaiters never occurred to me until I actually started to run in the sand dunes and by then it was too late, the damage was done. I did manage to improvise and use Tubigrip™®. Now gaiters are the norm and come in all shapes sizes and colours. I wore a run of the mill T-shirt, now specialist brands like Raidlight™® offer desert-proof running tops, incorporating sun and sand protection, now there is a huge market for technical clothing. Companies like Camelbak™® solve the water bottle carrying problem with the bladder/straw combination. Shoes, another area that has seen major improvements. Specialist shoes for running in every kind of environment, brand names like Icebug™® for, you've guessed it running on ice, Uk Gear™® sell a shoe especially designed for desert running. Salomon™®, Inov8™® and Walsh™®, there is a shoe for every kind of terrain. At the end of the day, the super-duper improvements that have been made to kit in recent years certainly make things a little more comfortable, but completing an Ultra distance race is still about putting one foot in front of the other for a very long time!

By nature I am a technophobic Luddite. I hate the office

environment, phones, computers, e-mails, blogs, etc. The pleasure I get from participating in an Ultra Distance race is priceless, the peace, quiet, tranquillity and solitude is a large part of why I choose to race in places such as the desert, jungle, mountain and Arctic. Unfortunately, modern day monstrosities known as Cyber Tents have recently appeared in certain stage races.

Not so very long ago, office workers would work away, tapping away at a keyboard, staring intently at a computer screen. E-mails, texts and blogs that all need answering as does the ever- present ringing telephone. Workers, wishing the day to end so that running kit can be donned and legs stretched, lungs filled with fresh air, out on a well-earned relaxing run. Now the introduction of Cyber Tents, tents that are really nothing more than mobile offices. The runner that has spent a small fortune and travelled thousands of miles to some beautiful remote part of the world to, no doubt, get away from the humdrum daily grind of office life by taking on a wonderfully tough challenge, that same runner spends the day experiencing a beautiful, peaceful, challenging run, only to finish each day looking forward to a trip to the office aka, the Cyber Tent so that they can send texts, e-mails and write blogs.

Whatever next, Virtual Ultras?

Chapter 12
Miscellaneous

At the time of writing this book, I have been racing Ultra Distance Races for a little over twenty years. There are still many races that I would still love to do. The reasons for me wanting to do even more races are varied. There are, of course, places I would love to visit. A new race in Papua New Guinea has recently been added to the Ultra races scene and has grabbed my attention. I would love to race in Antarctica, Australia, New Zealand and the Far East.

There are races in America that have also caught my eye, races like the Western States 100, the Leadville 100 and the Hardrock 100. I've looked at them and even thought about having a bash but something always stops me entering.

I like to race and I like to push and challenge myself. I also, as I mentioned earlier, enjoy the solitude, the fact that it is me and only me that pushes myself forward. When I'm tired, injured, hungry, thirsty, frightened or lost, it's me and my own mental tenacity that pushes me on. When and if I manage to reach the finish line, I can finally appreciate my own private battle, relish and reflect upon what I had to endure to reach that finish line.

Unfortunately, however, a lot of the races in America seem to encourage, or at least condone, the use of pace makers. These pacemakers are like lifejackets thrown to a drowning man. The drowning man that's floundering, struggling to keep his head above water, exhaustion and the will to keep going and just as he is about to go under for the last time, he is suddenly thrown a lifejacket and it saves the day.

I've had races where I'm hanging on by the skin of my teeth. Where I have seriously thought that I'm out of my depth, (no pun intended) I'm never going to make it, what on earth and never again, but somehow I manage to keep myself moving forward, my personal, private glory is all the more because it's mine and mine alone, no one did it for me. The thought of a pacemaker horrifies me, the metaphorical lifejacket there to help encourage and cajole, a clear head and a fresh pair of legs taking some of the workload.

I remember when I reached the Scroggie Creek checkpoint during the 2011 Yukon Arctic Ultra 430 mile, I was only allowed to proceed with the next runner, we had to travel together. I had to wait 15 hours for the next runner to appear. However, I understood the reasons why, the weather, deep snow and -45/50 degree temperatures, a couple of mountains, the race director made the right call. I accepted it but didn't like it, I had always raced and trained on my own, to have someone there was annoyingly intrusive – the difference was that we had both at that point been racing for days and had covered roughly 300 miles, in other words we were both equally knackered. We were in the same boat and had covered the same ground and were equal in ability and, as it turned out, equal in our distaste for travelling with another person.

Another thing that I have noticed over the years is that during a single stage race, it is rare that the top finishers are at the front of the start line – they are usually the quiet guys or girls tucked away at the back and they slowly manage to creep their way forward, free from the hustle and bustle, the jostling for the lead. When I started taking part in Ultras, my natural instinct was to get to the front and save precious seconds, seconds in a race that may well last several days of nonstop racing is pretty pointless. During the Yukon Arctic Ultra 430 mile race, I managed second place, the guy in front of me had beaten me not by seconds, minutes or even hours. He beat me by a couple of days, likewise during the 6633 ultra I won the race and the next guy was 11 hours behind.

Chapter 13
A few things I've learnt along the way!

Though I've been Ultra distance running for a little over 20 years, I'm only now just about getting the hang of it.

It's inevitable that over the years my speed has decreased, I'm a lot slower than I used to be (I was never particularly fast) however the missing 'speed' has now been replaced by patience, tolerance and the ability to endure and suffer, far more than I ever used to.

In the sport of Ultra Distance running it's the ability to endure, be patient and tolerate a large degree of suffering that are far more beneficial than mere speed.

Food Fest

Ultra distance running is just one big excuse to eat whatever you like, whenever you like, (well I can) Those in the know, would suggest that you must, as a runner of ultra long distances eat the proper and correct food, because the food you eat will really to be used as fuel.

Carbohydrates, fats, proteins, vitamins, various minerals, etc are all essential for the physically active, however and whilst I fully appreciate and respect those learned views, it doesn't help when you are traipsing through the Arctic or some Desert or other with a complete loss of appetite or worse your stomach really can't handle what the 'experts have recommended, no I have learnt to eat what I fancy, my body tells me what it needs, plodding along when a sudden craving for something like, chocolate, Pringles crisps, beef jerky, shortbread biscuits or mints, certainly during an Arctic race these 'junk food' items would be in my sledge, I would sooner eat crap food than no food, basically get anything down that you can keep down during the race and the fact that you are usually training reasonably hard means (for me anyway) that you can eat whatever you like and lots of it.

Starting Position

Another thing that I have learnt, is that it is best to start a long race such as an ultra, right at the back. I've started at the front in a couple of races and those of us standing there at the front grinning like Cheshire cats, make for a wonderful photograph, however the cheesy grins don't last long when the proper runners come tanking past and your ego kicks in, as you try not to let too many more people pass, you do what you must and speed up, using a pace that you can't realistically maintain and before long you're bolloxed your ego has now been deflated by the simple fact that so many people have passed you.

I now try and start at the back, realising that it is easier to slowly and methodically catch someone and hopefully work my way slowly through the field or use someone too latch onto and pull me along.

If you are at the front or near the front, which, believe it or not I've managed to do on a couple of occasions, the pressure is immense the feeling of being chased, hunted down, caught or overtaken makes life very unpleasant. A slow creep forward from the back is far more preferable than the fear of being chased.

Checkpoints: Friend or Foe

Checkpoints can unfortunately be as unhelpful as they are helpful. Brilliant for re-fueling, rehydrating and rest, they can also provide a welcome and often much needed boost to morale. However the temptation to linger for just a few more minutes, take advantage of pleasant company, comfy chairs, warm drinks etc can have the disadvantage of tricking the weary runner into making a silly decision, the blisters that hurt the muscles that ache and the distance yet to cover, the thought of getting back out onto the trail and continue with the monotonous miles they all conspire against you and you start to think that maybe going no further isn't such a bad idea, you start to convince yourself that you gave it your best shot and it would be silly to put yourself through more 'suffering' just for a medal and a T shirt, no, get the hell out of there, get moving, get away form the checkpoint.

Bite Size Chunks

When I stand at the start line of a race, I don't aim for the finish line I aim for the next checkpoint, I use it and leave it and when I leave it I aim for the next checkpoint and then the next, for me to aim for the finish line would be counter productive, the finish line could be hundreds of miles away, days away or just to bloody far away, an unreachable imaginary point, where as the next checkpoint is at least within reach and an achievable target.

Fitness

Fitness and training are obviously important, however the fittest guy on the start line is not necessary the guy who wins the race.

Mental toughness is far more important and certainly more of an asset than physical fitness.

With extreme races in extreme environments such as the Arctic, preparation and organisation are the absolute key to success, a super fit athlete who is unprepared and disorganised is unlikely to get very far.

Kit

We all love a bit of fancy kit, how many times have I been caught by my ever exasperated wife sneaking a peep at really fancy, expensive piece of must have kit, whilst on the computer, Kit is great and has, in the last few years come along way. It's a great talking point, looks good and is often the envy of others, whilst it makes life just a little more comfortable, however, having said all that, it's still down to the individual to grind out the miles, one step at a time and those poor sods that have become reliant on kit, come to a grinding halt when said piece of fancy kit, is broken or damaged the batteries have run out or is just plain not performing the way the sales person said it would.

Relaxing

When I say to friends or family that I find running relaxing, they look at me with, what can be best described as pity, bemusement and horror, after all running is hard work and unpleasant we all remember the fact that we were forced to take part in the humiliating school cross country run, black plimsoles, runny noses, red legs and the fast kids running off, not only leaving you behind but leaving you slightly humiliated and embarrassed.

Even now I find half marathons and marathons 'hard work' mainly because I'm not running at my 'relaxing' pace, a pace that is usually only found during ultras, a long slow comfortable plod and luckily for me sedate plodding is my speciality.

That's the simple beauty of an ultra, there is no pressure to 'run' fast, the knack is to plod slow and the longer the race the slower the plod or should I say 'the longer the race, the slower the pace' I can assure you either is very pleasant and very relaxing, you are less likely to get injured at a relaxed pace and you certainly have more time to ponder, the meaning of life.

Intimidation

Even now after all these years, I turn up at races and very often feel intimidated by the super, lean athletic looking, confidant athletes, that I have had the audacity to be in the same race as.

It's all to easy to feel like a fish out of water at some super race venue, with a professional looking crew, adorned in kit brandishing race logo, everyone else looks as if they know what they are doing, athletes wearing the latest gear, old hands swapping stories of last years race, old friends and allies reminiscing about last years race

I have also done enough races to realise the confidant guy, who is happily telling anyone that will listen, whilst wearing an ultra race finishers T shirt, all about previous epic races, tales of battles fought and won, injuries sustained, the recent training regime and the super benefits of his recently acquired brand new, fancy, must have piece kit, is not the guy to either listen too or be intimidated by, he's quite possibly trying to convince himself that he's better than he is or indeed better than you are, the physique that's been finally honed, sculptured and defined in the gym, will in all likelihood be not a lot of use, once proper food and sleep have been denied, the relentless miles that still need grinding out, no it's the mind, and the will to push on that gets you across the finish line. The quiet guy with well used and well thought out kit, the guy I've only just noticed standing somewhere near the back of the pack is usually the one who not only finishes, but usually finishes well.

Marathon of the Sands

Possibly the worlds most famous Extreme race on the planet 'The Marathon Des Sables'

This was my first race ever and my introduction to the world of Ultra distance running, I loved the thought of doing it, suffered and hated it when doing it and was ecstatic bordering on euphoric when I finished.

I was lucky the whole race was in those days much smaller in size not the huge enterprise it seems to have now become.

There are however better Desert races there are cheaper Desert races, harder desert races, easier desert races, races that are longer and races that are a damn sight more challenging, however the 'Marathon Des Sables' is the T shirt and medal that everyone wants, why?

The 'Marathon Des Sables' is undoubtedly a magical race, after all it worked it's magic on me, turning a thirty something lazy git into an Ultra distance runner (well sort of) and turning itself into a huge business/brand name.

It's a sport for others

It's really not, it's a sport for the 'everyman' The world of Ultra distance running is full of people like you and me, the simple fact of the matter is that every one of us that takes part, decided, for what ever reason, to have a go.

The reasons are many, for me it was just a one off adventure to see if I could run across a Desert, we all have our reasons for giving it a go, those reasons are often dressed up as, raising money for charity, because a group of friends are doing it, curiosity, personal challenge, bravado, ego, whatever the reason, give a go, you won't regret it, but you may well regret not giving it a go, what have you got to lose, except maybe a few toe nails, even then, those are worn with pride and bragged about.

There's a great poem by the Irish poet William F. O'Brien that sums up the 'regret' of not having a bash.

Better to try and fail than never to try at all

Some say risk nothing, try only for the sure thing,
Others say nothing gambled nothing gained,
Go all out for your dream.
Life can be lived either way, but for me,
I'd rather try and fail, than never try at all. you see.

Some say "Don't ever fall in love,
Play the game of life wide open,
Burn your candle at both ends."
But I say "No it's better to have loved and lost,
Than never to have loved at all, my friend."

When many moons have gone by,
And you are alone with your dreams of yesteryear,
All you memories will bring you cheer.
You'll be satisfied, succeed or fail, win or lose,
Knowing the right path you did choose.

William F. O'Brien
1852-1928

In other words, go on give it a bash!

The Runner's Nuts

Chapter 14
Rovaniemi 150

What is it: A Winter Ultra Marathon

When: February

Where: Northern Finland

Distance: 66 km, 150 km or 300 km

It is: A great introduction to cold weather, winter races

See: www.rovaniemi150.com

Landing at Rovaniemi Airport and the first thing that I noticed that it was warm, well, warm that is for what was after all, supposed to be an Arctic Race. With the temperature hovering around zero degrees it was, I decided officially the warmest cold weather race I had been too.

I had, had the foresight to pre book my taxi and was impressed when I was met by a dour looking rotund individual. After placing my one piece of luggage into the back of his car, he without so much as a hello, how are you, reluctantly allowed me in to his chariot, after confirming that I was to be taken to the Hotel Pohavajomini we were off.

A short 20 minute ride was all that it took. I made my way over to reception. Unfortunately for me, the receptionist looked as if she was having a bad day, stern and angry looking, it was only when I gave my name and explained that I had a reservation did she actually smile and became helpful, friendly and more than happy to help, until that was she informed that there was no reservation for me at this Hotel. On further checking she found that I was actually staying at the Hotel Pohavajomani, Polar Rooms!

Me, being not the brightest of sparks, obviously, thought it was the same Hotel but I had opted for the Polar Rooms, oh no two different Hotels with a similar name.

She went on to give directions a quick walk through town and it was just a few hundred meters away, I of course instantly looked to see if my taxi was still there, it wasn't.

Bollox, traipsing through town carrying 25 kilos of luggage looking for a Hotel, things had not got off to a great start.

The following morning it was the dreaded kit inspection, I always hate these, they make me nervous, like having to sit an exam, the fear of some jobsworth kit inspector, getting all excited and finicky , sorry sir you should have bought this, you shouldn't have that, you forgot the thingy ma bob, that's the wrong colour and this needs replacing etc, etc, I needn't have worried, it was a simple case of checking that I had bought the sleeping bag I said I was going to bring, I had the required headlight plus spare batteries and a whistle, I passed.

Alex, the race organiser is, it would be fair to say enthusiastic, he explained that he actually came up with the idea for the Rovaniemi150 after taking part in the famous Iditarod Trail Invitational (see www.iditarodtrailinvitational.com) a race in Alaska, he realised that there was no similar race in Europe and wanted to afford others the opportunity to experience what was once only available in Canada, Alaska or the States (I know the States and Alaska are supposedly one and the same, well, on paper, at least.) using the same format with different distances and three different forms of self propelled locomotion, i.e. Ski, bike or foot he came up with this race, which is designed to be a great 'introduction' to Winter Ultra Distance racing.

I entered this race because as per usual, for me, it's where the race is, not what the race is, I had wanted to visit Finland for some time and with the distance of only 150 km or just a little over 90 miles, it wasn't to be a logistical nightmare. I was now an experienced cold weather racer, ergo I would surely finish, (famous last words, that would come back to haunt me). The whole race would only involve a long weekend away and the cost was not astronomical unlike some Canadian/American races.

Once the pre race briefing was over, it was off to the Hotel for a good nights sleep. The following morning, there was just a short walk to the start line, down on the local river.

The usual overly excited loud chatter, the race organiser desperately trying to get everyones attention with last minute details, athletes adorned in multi coloured kit, being checked for the umpteenth time, photos being taken, shared and shown, a drone flying a few meters taking pictures and filming, above grabbed everyones attention we all instinctively waved and shouted at it.

As the ten second countdown began, a serious and sudden silence made it's presence felt, the proverbial calm before the storm.

Three, two, one and we are off, the cyclists shooting off, keen to take advantage of the fact that we were on a flat ice covered river, the skiers desperately untangling poles and skies and trying to find a steady rhythm and then us, the pulk pulling so called runners.

Just ten minutes after starting I looked up and was surprised to see so many people so far ahead, it was possibly the fastest start to a cold weather race I had ever seen.

During the Yukon Arctic Ultra (see www.arcticultra.de) the race starts on a single small path beside the mighty Yukon River, it is virtually impossible to over take anyone for the first couple of kms, which is great if only because it keeps everyone in check and affords the opportunity to slowly warm up and get the body going, by the time you hit the river and the chance to speed up you are prepped , warmed up and ready to go. The 6633 ultra (see www.6633ultra.com) is also a slow start but that is usually because everyone is terrified.

I, like a complete and utter TIT, chose to ignore myself and some how got carried along with the speedy racers (I always tell anyone and everyone who asks, go at your own pace, don't, what ever you do, get carried away and go to fast early on)

Before to long I was pulling myself off, of the river to checkpoint 1. I should have been pleased with the remarkable time, but no I was sweating, with drops of perspiration dripping off me and whilst signing myself in I noticed rather alarmingly that my gloves were steaming, this did not bode well and I knew it, unfortunately however I, also like a complete Twat ignored it!

Once off the river bank and back onto the river, I carried on at my stupidly fast pace.

Usually when I race and particularly early on in a race, I lock onto someone, I see them up ahead and refuse to let them out of my sight, sometimes this works and they inadvertently help by dragging me along and sometimes it back fires on me, I was now beginning to think that on this occasion it was starting to back fire, but none the less I carried on.

Following the contours of the river and keeping an eye on the person ahead, I noticed that the route took them to the left, this was confirmed when I reached a member of the race crew sitting on a stationery snow machine, he was giving clear instructions, for those racers that were doing the 66 km distance had to go the right and the others to the left, he also informed me that the next check point was just 5 km away.

A short time after leaving him, it was off the river and up into the forest, it took a little effort to get off the river and rather annoyingly I was still having to work too hard, in my desperation to keep the runner in front in sight. (Bloody Ego)

I was still sweating and drinking far more than I was expecting, sweating in these conditions is never wise and it's the one thing you should never do, if only because the moment you slow down or stop there is a very real fear of the sweat freezing, damp clothing is to be avoided at all cost. I was a little concerned but had already decided that I was going at a pace I was unable to maintain, so would slow down after the next checkpoint and I hoped that as a bonus the slowing down to a more sensible/

sustainable pace might, just might dry out my damp clothing.

Traipsing through the forest is nearly always enjoyable, it's a truly beautiful, almost magical place, snow covered trees, seemingly sculptured into surreal shapes, the heavy weight of snow covered branches were being forced into strange unnatural contortions, the imagination, especially when bored or tired sets to work morphing the ordinary snow covered branch into something other than reality, strange mythical creatures, vehicles and buildings all seem to be here in the forest. Anything and everything is seen, everything that is, but the bloody checkpoint, the only thing you want to see, never seems to appear and then without warning it's there, nothing fancy just a couple of people, a small fire and some water.

Water was the only thing I needed, so I quickly filled my Nalgene bottle, signed in and left, but not before I was given a friendly piece of advice, the next kilometre was going to be tricky and there will be a small, a very small narrow bridge to cross. Tricky was an understatement, a tight narrow path just about a body width wide, sharp tight bends, made manoeuvrability all but impossible, I had no choice but take my harness off, push the connecting poles back over the sledge grab the front of the sledge and sort of man handle the thing around the very tight bends, even then the sledge was just a bit to bloody long, to negotiate the very tight turns, I was having to work hard and plan each and every step, weaving my way through as opposed to walking my way through and the fact that I kept knocking branches that were covered in snow which of course meant that every so often I dislodged a load of snow from the upper branches and consequently I got a dusting or several, funny to any one watching and bloody annoying for me, then I spotted it, or rather I spotted someone trying to get themselves and sledge across what was euphemistically called a bridge it appeared to be more of a tight rope than a bridge.

The guy in front was struggling and his sledge was far more compact than mine, his was a short sledge stacked higher than mine, where as mine was much longer but packed flat, once he was safely across, it was my turn, I carefully manoeuvred my sledge around the last of the trees stepped onto the bridge, I was to all in tense in purposes *'Slack lining' carefully watching each of my steps on the slippery snow/ice covered wood, whilst being mesmerised by the moving water just a meter or so below, then disaster, my sledge would not move it was stuck fast, edged between two small trees, I couldn't afford to pull to hard lest I slip and slide into the water, I gently pulled and oh so gently teased my sledge around and then it happened just as I freed the thing a combination of a steep snow covered river bank and gravity saw the front of my sledge slide into the water, the guy in front realised I had made a complete tit of things and could not move, he came to my assistance and pulled the front of my sledge up onto the bridge, when I was finally lined up and good to go I thanked him, he shot off, no doubt laughing and then I finally reached the other side.

Once I was across I scooped out the wet slushy snow from the front of my sledge and then unzipped my sled bag checked the inside for any water damage, fortunately the sled bag was as water proof as I had been told and there was nothing inside the bag that had got wet.

Wet kit and wet food in these conditions would be an absolute night mare. Satisfied that all was good I harnessed up and buggered off, it was only a short while before the maze like forest ended and it was once more onto a frozen lake.

As a treat for surviving the forest of doom, tight rope walking across the bridge of sighs and dunking the sledge, I had a quick cup of coffee and a mouth full of my old favourite, Rolo's.

*Slacklining: Is basically 'Tight Rope' walking using 'Webbing' instead of 'Rope'

At home a simple cup of coffee and a couple of rolo's, doesn't really mean that much however during a race like this, the simple coffee, rolo combination becomes one of life's great experiences a moment to savour and a moment to look forward too, it was whilst savouring that particular moment, that suddenly and out of the blue I inexplicability decided to go the whole hog and have a fudge finger, hang the expense I say.

After ten minutes I started to get cold, so decided to get my arse in gear and get moving. We were now on yet another lake, which was a blessed relief from having to fight my way through the maze like obstacle course that the organiser's had euphemistically called a forest. Because I had taken just a little to long faffing about with coffee and chocolate I could now feel the cold trying to creep in, I decided to push on hard and fast whilst on the lake, taking full advantage of it's flatness. It didn't take long to feel the warmth returning which felt good, what was not so good was that I was beginning to have that familiar unpleasant feeling of impending doom, CHAFFING, it felt like I was attempting to smuggle sandpaper through customs, sandpaper which I had rather cleverly secreted between the cheeks of my arse, it was only now that remembered that I had not Sudocremed. Bollox, why, oh why had I not bothered to Sudocrem my nether regions, I had spent ages putting Bodyglide* on my feet, I usually have a pre race ritual that involves Bodyglide and Sudocrem** and yet for some bizarre reason I had neglected my nether regions, I never neglect my nether regions, I'm rather fond of my nether regions in fact I would go as far to say I love my nether regions and I know from bitter experience that neglected nether regions in an Ultra race, can never be a good thing and will only ever end in tears!

Too late now, I'll just have to grin and bare it

Plodding along, pondering on the impending doom, awaiting my Gluteus Maximas, I spotted what appeared to be a runner or runners that seemed to have stopped and as per usual this was my cue to up the anti, slowly increasing my limited speed to see if I could catch up and possibly with a little luck and with the wind in the right direction, fingers crossed etc, over take them, as I drew level it became clear that it was two knackered looking cyclists, these two were having a breather, the deep snow was making life unpleasant for cyclists in general and inexperienced cyclists in particular, they also had a type of bike that I had never seen before, usually the bikes in these races are called 'Fatback' bikes specially designed with super wide wheels, these were, what can only be described as 'articulated' bikes, huge 'Fatback' bikes with a trailer attached, it looked from a distance like a very long three wheeled bike, I didn't envy them, the effort required to pull, push and drag them through the deep snow and maze like forest, must have been enormous, plus, I learnt a long time ago, to only ever take a small pack, because if you take a big one, you tend to fill it, now with a trailer attached the temptation to over pack the thing had apparently been unavoidable.

We looked and smiled at each other and I carried on, pleased with the fact that I had caught someone and again that question, why, why do I get so much pleasure in catching some one, I'm never trying to win a race or break records, I enter to finish, to see if I can reach the finish line and yet, given the smallest of opportunities to catch, overtake or beat some one I will. If I was in a race like the London Marathon, where some 30,000 people shoot off from the start line, I could be possibly be number 15,960 with 14 miles to go, I see someone ahead slowing down so I instinctively have to speed up, only making my super human often painful effort worth it, because of the fact that I'm now 15,959!!!

Eventually the lake ends and I soon found myself approaching the next checkpoint, again the plan is to stop for the absolute minimum, a quick top up of water, which I'm still drinking at an alarming rate. The checkpoint though basic, looks all to inviting, with it's fire, happy, helpful crew and even happier relieved racers, I'm surprised to see so many bikers, but the going has been awful the snow, soft, deep and uneven is making everyones progress slow, conscious of the strict cut offs and the fact that I'm as per usual not wearing a watch, I'm fearful of falling behind, I need to keep moving in case the conditions deteriorate.

I leave after just a few minutes. Shortly after leaving I finally decide to put on my snow shoes, last time I wore these was during the Yukon Arctic Ultra in 2011 I remember what a difference they made, walking on the snow instead of through the snow, now I've got them on I'm realising that I should have put them on much, much earlier, the difference is instant, they are, if nothing else a real labour saving device.

The type of snowshoes I was wearing were called Yowies* a snowshoe from of all places Australia. I've used them before and loved the fact that they are not only really easy to use causing no real change in the way I move, but are quick to put on and remove, they do , like me, look big, awkward and clumsy, but they are fantastic pieces of kit.

After an hour or so, I spotted another runner up ahead, they had stopped and were faffing about and I of cause did my usual mercenary trick and made an effort to take full advantage, it must have taken 20 minutes or so before I realised that he was actually trying to put on a pair of snowshoes, but he seemed to be making a complete 'pigs ear' of it, unlike my Yowies which were idiot friendly, he seemed to be having all sorts of problems, why, I wondered had he not bothered to practise, now was not the time to learn, I thought, what a pillock, that would teach him and for a moment I felt smug and then a right TWAT when I drew level, the guy only had one arm and was having to do a two armed fiddly job, in the cold, I felt ashamed, I asked if he was ok, he said he was and I slopped off.

Approaching the next checkpoint, I was again surprised by how many people were here and the cyclists seemed to out number the runners. The fire was just too tempting, I was for some reason beginning to feel the strain, the pace was a little to fast, I had been sweating far more than I should have been, I was drinking far more than I should have been and my feet were cold, this was confusing because I was warm, too warm, but my feet weren't.

I couldn't work out why, I've raced hundreds, upon hundreds of miles in Arctic conditions, conditions far, far colder than this, but never had cold feet. I was using the same shoe, sock combination, Salomon XA Pro GTX shoes with 'Sealskinz' thermal socks, with a merino wool lining

I grabbed a seat and as soon as my arse touched the thing was reminded in no uncertain terms that chaffing had made it's unwelcome appearance.

There is I decided something rather special about a large open fire in a night time, winter wonderland, warm, welcoming, orange flames, dancing and casting flickering shadows a complete contrast to it's surroundings, cold, still and often unwelcoming, it was comforting, cosy and just to bloody tempting, it's so easy to have 'just another five minutes' With this in mind I shoved the last of my shortbread biscuits in my mouth, finished off my cup of coffee and got the hell out there.

Back on the trail and peace and quiet. My attention was again drawn to the fact that my feet were cold. I decided to put my Neo's** on, these overshoes would afford another layer of warmth for my feet.

YOWIE:* The snowshoe is named after Australias very own 'Big Foot' A mythical creature reputed to live in the Australian wilderness.

Neo's: ** These are a light weight water proof overshoe, that protect footwear from water and cold.

Once happy it was back to plodding, I could see no one up ahead and I hadn't the bottle to look behind, because if I did, I would of undoubtedly been disappointed that I was, one, being chased and two, my head torch would have given the game away, to whom ever was behind, they would think I was struggling (I was but I certainly didn't want to advertise the fact!) and give chase, well, that's what I would do if the person in front looked around at me.

I tried to work out the distances between check points, because as usual I wasn't really paying attention, during the pre race briefing and not being a clever soul I usually have to simplify things, so instead of trying to memorise the distances between each of the checkpoints, I just noted that there were eight checkpoints, I was now heading toward checkpoint four, ergo, I was halfway.

I was nearly happy with my simplified version of reality, when I remembered that the distance between checkpoint six and seven was huge at about 34 kms.

I was still trying to get my head around the fact that, I thought 34 kms was huge, in this race it was, but in the great scheme of things it wasn't, during a race like the Yukon Arctic Ultra, the first checkpoint is also the shortest distance at 42 kms.

Checkpoint four appeared and again I did what I needed to do, collected water and left, determined to make full use of the fact that I still felt strong and fresh. The psychological advantage of knowing that I left a checkpoint whilst people who had arrived before me were still there is always good, I've done races before where I have struggled to keep up with some one, they have reached a checkpoint 15/20 minutes before me and in my rather ruthless determination to grab an advantage even it was only a short term psychological one, I arrive collect water and leave, hoping that they then think I'm strong and fresh and decide to say bollox, I'll let him go, he's to strong, the reality is I'm in all likely hood having a break a mile or so up the trail.

I know it seems a contradiction or even hypocritical when I try to catch someone up, but then I have the gall to say I'm not trying to win.

I don't set out to win, but I do set out to do my best, I try and reach the finish line as quickly as I can and the little games of catching other racers is just that, a game something to help with the sometime monotonous nature of this type of racing. I certainly wouldn't chase down one of the racing snakes, it takes all my effort to do my best and reach the end.

Checkpoint five soon arrived and again I was determined to keep moving after topping up with more water and getting confirmation from the support crew that the next checkpoint was the best with the chance to get inside a small hut, warm up and get ready for the 34 km stretch that would get me to the penultimate checkpoint seven.

After another quick turn around it was back onto the trail, I was in the process of giving myself a mental once over, just checking that everything was fine, I had enough food, a small flask of coffee and a larger flask of hot water, I felt good no aches, no pain except a rather irritating chaffing, but I'd had worse, I wasn't tired or sleepy, was eating and drinking ok, however I was thirsty but was keeping on top of it, by constantly sipping from my camelbak which had an electrolyte solution drink in and occasional sips from my 'nalgene' bottle which contained water and now that I had settled down to a sensible pace, I was no longer over heating I felt comfortable, except for my feet, both were cold but my right one more so. I was still trying to work out why my feet were cold when I remembered 'frostbite'. During the 2011 430 mile Yukon Arctic Ultra I had stupidly allowed my feet to get frostbitten, a combination of tiredness and rank stupidity allowed me to make a silly mistake or two (I also managed to get frost bite on my ear) I was lucky then and was told in no uncertain terms that if I ever allowed my feet to freeze again I could well end up losing bits and pieces, now that warning was playing heavily on my mind.

I don't mind being in pain, I don't mean to say I'm some sort of masochist happily inflicting pain for some rather perverted pain/pleasure combo, but rather I except it and am, to a large degree able to tolerate it, however I would never intentionally push myself so hard that permanent physical damage is done, purely to reach the finish line of a race.

I was weighing all this up when I finally reached checkpoint six, this was considered the best checkpoint, the only one that had a small log cabin with heating in.

I dropped off my pulk and made my way inside, there were about 10 people inside all sat around a large log fire which was in the centre, a couple were trying to sleep, some were eating and drinking and some looked as if they had no intention of leaving. I grabbed a seat, which was on top of a jerry can, poured myself a coffee, the plan was to have a good longish break before tackling the next 34 km section, however after ten minutes or so I could feel myself getting comfortable, getting warm and getting tired, time to bugger off, but I was in a dilemma, my feet, what was happening to my feet was I damaging them, would they last or were they just cold, I couldn't decide what to do. I weighed everything up, they were working (for now) and I was at a checkpoint, I've always promised myself that I would never give up, at a checkpoint, I would always push on to the next one, decision made, feet were working and get the hell out of the checkpoint so I ventured out and pushed on.

Back onto the trail and into the unknown, I plodded and pondered, I was alone and concerned about my feet, if they could just hold out until the next checkpoint, I had no idea what time it was, couldn't gauge my speed, all I knew was that I was going far slower than I normally go.

I was sort of comfortable, warm but not hot, wasn't hungry or thirsty my sled didn't feel heavy and my feet had stopped being cold, in fact my feet didn't feel anything, I literally couldn't feel them. Was this better than them being cold, I wasn't sure, but as long as they didn't hurt and I was relatively comfortable I would push on.

One thing I did notice was that I was becoming clumsy, occasionally tripping over my snowshoes, tiredness must have crept up on me.

Eventually the trail disappeared and a road took it's place, daylight appeared and at last I could take the snow shoes off. I figured that with the snow shoes off and the fact that I was now on a proper road during daylight hours I would be able to pick up a bit of speed.

The best laid plans and all that, ensured that I still just plodded along, tripping over my feet, which were still not co operating and giving me cause for concern, I now wished that they were suffering with the cold or blistered, at least I would have felt something the not feeling my feet was worrying me, worrying me enough to pull over, have a drink of warm chocolate a few shortbread biscuit and a quick look at my feet, however I didn't even get to remove a shoe, I didn't have too to know that they were swollen.

I knew better than to remove my shoes, because if I did, the swelling would increase to such an extent that there would be no way on earth I'd be able to get my shoes back on.

Numb and swollen, not a great combination, however I could use them and still move forward and if I could just reach the next checkpoint, checkpoint seven was the last one, from there it was a relatively short hop to the finish line back in Rovaniemi

So for now, it was time to do what I do best, head down, man up and move off. Moving along the road, over a bridge and across a round about, I felt ok and thought I was moving at a reasonable pace until that was, I got over taken by three people in relatively quick succession, the annoying thing was, not the fact that I had been overtaken, but that I was not able to do a thing about it, they just seem to pull away.

Eventually I spotted a car that belonged to the support crew, they pointed me in the right direction which was a sharp left hand turn, I must have looked as bad as my feet felt because, because one member of the support crew said, 'don't worry it's just eight km until the next checkpoint'

Again for some bizarre reason I thanked him, reapplied my stiff upper lip and trundled off. After a few 100 meters there was a right hand turn that took me off the road and onto the trail proper, once I got off the road I had a quick look behind, to see if anyone was coming, they weren't the coast was clear, so it was off with the harness and time for coffee.

Then just as I was deciding what to do about my feet, ie: check to see if they were still there and if they were, what damage had been done, when a cyclist appeared, the usual exchange of pleasantries, he asked if I was ok, I of course lied and said 'yep, everything is fine, just having a five minute break and then he shot off.

After my interrupted tea break I harnessed up and moved off, annoyed that I wasn't able to have five minutes peace and quiet, strange considering I had virtually been on my own since the race started.

After what I guessed to be an hours or so, the trail turned to the right onto a long narrow path and looking ahead I could see the cyclist that had interrupted my tea break. walking and pushing his bike, being the annoying git that I can so often be, I decided to catch him up, see how he likes it thought. Childish and pointless I know, but I was suffering, my feet were giving me real cause for concern and the fact that I was to scared to have a look at them, meant that I was glad of this little distraction.

The fact that he was pushing an awkward looking bike packed with panniers, through soft snow, up a slight incline in cycling shoes meant that I was sure to catch him, I did, and when I did, I didn't feel any better, especially as he turned out to be a really nice bloke. We plodded along together for a while, not really talking that much owing to a slight language barrier, then as the slight incline levelled out he was suddenly on his bike and cycling away.

After twenty minutes or so the trail took a sharp left hand turn and it was more of the same, a long well defined path, my feet were still numb, I guessed that the check point was roughly 5km away and if that was the case I would have approximately 35 km to go!

The same question popped into my head 'were my feet damaged and frost bitten' The strange thing about frostbite is that you don't feel it happening, not like a blister, where you get a 'hot spot' which is a sort of warning, a warning that is best listened to, it gives you the opportunity to stop and sort yourself out, frost bite is an injury you only know you have done, but don't actually know that you are doing, it's always too late when you realise and this was constantly playing on my mind, messing with my mojo, causing me concern.

That great Quote by Winston Churchill, 'never give in, never give in, never, never, never, in nothing, great or small, large or petty, never give in, except to convictions of honour and good sense'

I plodded along thinking about possible amputation, when I heard a snow machine approaching from behind, the driver stopped and told me I only had a couple of Km to go, I was mighty tempted to 'knock it on the head' and grab a lift, but with just a couple of km, decided to plod on.

As soon as the snow machine left I regretted my decision, what if my feet were frost bitten and black, what if I had now pushed my luck a little bit to far and once to often, I was, I decided a bloody fool and if by some miracle I get out of this in one piece with all digits accounted for I promise to never ever be so stupid again.

Then I caught the faint whiff of a log fire, log fires usually means checkpoints, I listened and became extra vigilant straining to confirm that a checkpoint was close and then I heard voices and the wonderful sight of a log fire with a couple of people savouring the warmth I recognised one as be the cyclist from earlier on.

The crew as usual were happy smiling and offering help, I grabbed a flask of coffee a seat and sat contemplating, 30 km to go. Could I make it, my feet were a major concern and played a large part in my final decision, with the Doctors words ringing in my ears, 'if you ever freeze them again, you'll LOSE THEM' 30 km was 30 km, too much I pulled the plug, with discretion being the better part of valour, maybe on this occasion, Churchill was right about giving in to Good Sense, I decided to live to fight another day, I've never been a gambler, and I wasn't about to start gambling with my feet, melodramatic I know, but I'm rather fond of my feet, and wanted to keep them.

I let the crew know of my decision and they organised the snow machine driver to take the two of us that had reached the same decision to the main road where we would be returning to the Hotel.

As soon as I reached the Hotel I phoned my wife to let her know that everything was ok, if she saw that I had withdrawn she would possibly think the worst (and no doubt check the insurance policy) My feet were fine, swollen, red and tender, but no blisters, no frost bite.

Within the week I had contacted the race organiser and booked my place for the following year, I hate not finishing and knowing that finishing the Rovaniemi 150 is more than possible I just had to return, BLOODY EGO!!!

Chapter 15
The Last Chapter

As I finish writing this book, I reflect on the last twenty years, twenty years' worth of adventurous challenges, I realise how very lucky I am.

The sport of Ultra Distance Running is one of the fastest-growing sports around, new races seem to appear almost weekly. In the UK, races like 'The Spine' and 'The Dragons Back' have quickly become classics, many more UK races are incredibly popular and are often oversubscribed, for example the famous 'Lakeland 100 mile Ultra' in the Lake District is filled to capacity minutes after registration is opened. The world famous 'Marathon Des Sables' with its enormous price tag of around £3000 is similarly filled within a few minutes of the registration opening.

So popular has the sport now become that some races such as the 'Marathon Des Sables' are brand names with merchandising, packs, bags, cups, mugs, T-shirts, caps and clothing, the Yukon Arctic Ultra has recently added its own special edition YAU fatback bike – a purpose-built bicycle, designed for cycling on the snowy and icy trails. DVDs and photographs are big business. I have clambered over many a sand dune or crawled into some isolated checkpoint to be met by a camera crew filming some documentary or a photographer glad to take your picture, if only because they have, in all probability, been hanging around bored and fed up and when a very knackered runner's sudden appearance breaks the monotony, it justifies the boredom and, of course, it's business

In the Uk magazines such as 'Like the Wind" and 'Ultra Magazine' have hit the market, a plethora of books such as the one you are reading have also hit the market, specialist shops, kit websites and training camps have all recently been created to encourage/ capitalise on the burgeoning Ultra Racing scene.

Why is such a physically demanding, time-consuming sport so popular? I think that a lot of the Ultra's appeal seems to be, that for many (me included) an Ultra race is not a race, it's a challenge, a challenge against yourself and a challenge against the course,. Rarely do you line up with someone aiming for a specific time. PBs and Ultras don't sit well together, finishing eventually, is far more important than finishing in a specific time.

An Ultra allows you to run slowly and even walk without feeling silly. 10km, half-marathons etc don't afford the ego or pride the same luxury, or is it just me that feels that way?

Ultra Distance Running has given me so many things, it's given me the chance to travel the world, see and experience things and places rarely experienced by a 'mere tourist'. I have been fortunate indeed in meeting some amazing people, I have taken on challenges that I had considered were only for the elite sportsmen and women. I have pushed myself to the absolute limit and on a couple of occasions, I've pushed beyond those supposed limits, those so called 'limits' I now realise are nothing more than an imaginary line, a line that for whatever reason I had decided I was unable to go beyond, and yet I did.

I have, by way of a bonus, gained a level of fitness and confidence. The positives gained from Ultra distance running are many: the memories of places visited, checkpoints and finishing lines reached, people met and friends made – the list goes on. I have also noticed that those positives are long-lasting and often permanent (memories etc will always be there.) Kilian Jornet, widely regarded as the world's best 'Trail Runner' says *"All the bad things about running are there to reap something good."* In other words, it's worth it in the end.

On the other hand, I have learned that the negatives are short-term, things like blisters, pain, fatigue, hunger, thirst, apprehension and fear all, either, heal or pass.

The lessons learned (and the lessons that we have yet to learn) are vast, I know that pain is temporary and failure is forever. I also know that the human body is amazingly resilient and an incredibly adaptable tough 'tool.' However, the mind is all that and so much more.

I have also realised that the words FAIL and END are just acronyms, FAIL actually means First Attempt in Learning and END means Effort Never Dies. Dreams are really just targets to be aimed at and 'giving up' hurts like hell and the 'hurt' is permanent!

If you are thinking about having a bash – do it, I promise you won't ever regret having a bash: you might hate doing it, but you will, I assure you, love forever, having had a bash.

Acknowledgements

I would like to thank so many people without whom my Ultra running dreams and book-writing aspirations would remain just that: dreams.

The contents of this book owe a huge thank you to those people who gave permission to use and quote them, firstly, Mike Calvin and Dr Mike Stroud who unwittingly kickstarted the whole thing back in 1995 with their simple words of encouragement.

For allowing me to use and quote various pieces of written work and in no particular order – Tegyn Angel, Taylor Fleishner, Penelope Boettiger and Tanya Basu.

I would also like to take this opportunity to thank every single volunteer and race crew member that has manned all and any of the checkpoints that I have passed through during the last twenty years, my fellow Ultra distance running friends for making every race worth turning up for, the race organisers without whom the whole thing would not be possible and, of course, my wife Marilyn who has supported, helped and encouraged me every single step of the way, whilst I do the easy bit of leaving the start line and crossing the finish line (most of the time). She does the hard bits of supporting and waiting – for that I am eternally grateful and very fortunate indeed.

I would also like to say thank you the reader for reading my rather amateurish ramblings. I really do appreciate it.

I'm sure I've missed people out, but thank you all.

Also by the Author

'FARTLEKS and FLATULENCE'

Is David's first book, with over 3000 copies sold.

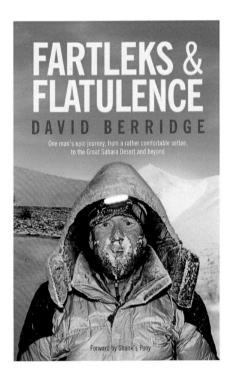

An often funny, brutality honest account of the author's participation in seventeen of the world's toughest challenges

Shortlisted for a 'National Media Award' in 2015.

(www.scottishadventureawards.com)

The Runner's Nuts